DISCARD

INFORMATION
FOR ACADEMIC LIBRARY
DECISION MAKING

Recent Titles in Contributions in Librarianship and Information Science
Series Editor: PAUL WASSERMAN

A Community Elite and the Public Library: The Uses of Information in
Leadership
Pauline Wilson

Public Knowledge, Private Ignorance: Toward a Library and Information
Policy
Patrick Wilson

Ideas and the University Library: Essays of an Unorthodox Academic
Librarian
Eli M. Oboler

Reform and Reaction: The Big City Public Library in American Life
Rosemary Ruling Du Mont

Acquisitions: Where, What, and How
Ted Grieder

Information Sources in Children's Literature: A Practical Reference Guide
for Children's Librarians, Elementary School Teachers, and Students of
Children's Literature
Mary Meacham

The Vital Network: A Theory of Communication and Society
Patrick Williams and Joan Thornton Pearce

Cogent Communication: Overcoming Reading Overload
Charles L. Bernier and Neil A. Yerkey

The Librarian's Psychological Commitments: Human Relations in
Librarianship
Florence E. DeHart

Organization Development for Academic Libraries: An Evaluation of the
Management Review and Analysis Program
Edward R. Johnson and Stuart H. Mann

Social Science Reference Sources: A Practical Reference Guide
Tze-chung Li

INFORMATION
FOR ACADEMIC LIBRARY
DECISION MAKING
The Case for Organizational
Information Management

CHARLES R. McCLURE

Contributions in Librarianship and Information Science, Number 31

Greenwood Press
Westport, Connecticut

Library of Congress Cataloging in Publication Data

McClure, Charles R
  Information for academic library decision making.

  (Contributions in librarianship and information science ;
no. 31 ISSN 0084-9243)
  Bibliography: p.
  Includes index.
    1. Libraries, University and college—Administration—
Decision-making. 2. Communication in library
administration. I. Title. II. Series.
Z675.U5M18   025.1   79-8412
ISBN 0-313-21398-4

Library of Congress Catalog Card Number: 79-8412
ISBN: 0-313-21398-4
ISSN: 0084-9243

First published in 1980

Greenwood Press
A division of Congressional Information Service, Inc.
88 Post Road West, Westport, Connecticut 06881

Printed in the United States of America

10 9 8 7 6 5 4 3 2 1

CONTENTS

FIGURES

Tables

PREFACE

During the past few years, librarians have been made aware of a stagnant state or at times a decrease in the monies made available to operate libraries. Administrators are responsible for obtaining increased funds as a means of improving the overall resources of the library; but acquired financial resources are only as effective as the decision process that allocates those resources and the ability of human resources in the library to utilize them.

My recent experiences in academic libraries—as well as with the data that are reported in this volume—suggest that these two areas are ones in which we can significantly improve administrative effectiveness. And, indeed, the link between the decision process and the utilization of human resources appears to be centered on a process that might be termed "information-handling ability." But the acquisition and transfer of information, internally and externally, by librarians *for purposes of decision making* have only recently received the attention of researchers.

One central theme of this volume is the importance of organizational information management. Clearly, we must be more concerned with the effective use of information resources as a means to improve the utilization of human resources and overall library decision making. At an organizational *and* personal level, librarians must manage information resources, analyze their information-handling ability, and develop strategies by which their decision making is based on accurate and timely information. Improved information handling and organizational information processing are two important results of information management.

This volume is a first step in the direction of exploring librarians' information acquisition and transfer within the academic library setting. But the context of this information acquisition and transfer is one of decision making. How is information *used* to make effective decisions regarding the library? Although this key question is addressed, it still remains to be answered and responses to it will continue to be controversial. If we can first explore what sources are contacted and how they are evaluated, perhaps we can better understand their utilization in the decision process. Ultimately, such research will suggest specific strategies to increase the effectiveness of resource allocation by administrators.

An apparent decrease in cooperation and mutual problem solving between the typical professional librarian and the library administrator is cause for considerable concern. Administrators find their credibility with staff reduced because of environmental factors over which they have little control, and the professional librarian "on the line" asserts that administrators have little contact with the reality of day-to-day problems that must be solved. For their part administrators comment that some librarians do not assume responsibility and simply do not understand "the big picture." And, of course, everyone simply lacks enough time to address all the issues that must be solved.

In such situations a gulf emerges between administration and "production." Data in this study reinforce the commonly held belief that administrators and librarians could improve their sharing and use of information sources. Moreover, a commonly held view that was informally mentioned numerous times to me while collecting the data was that (1) many librarians simply believe they have no *need* to acquire and disseminate information for purposes of decision making because there are few mechanisms to channel that information into the decision-making process, and (2) administrators tend to believe that most librarians have neither the desire nor the information to be actively involved in decision making.

The problem is less of determining blame and more of developing strategies by which administrators can attain the full benefit of the librarians' expertise, and all staff members can contribute to an effective decision-making process. A first step is to recognize the primary role of the professional librarian as a decision maker; the second is to recognize the incredible loss of resources when staff members are unable to make decisions because they cannot or do not possess accurate information. Thus, in a time of decreasing financial resources we must develop strategies to tap the full potential of the human resources in the library.

This volume does not pretend to answer all the questions regarding effective resource allocation through improved organizational information management. Although strategies are suggested, numerous propositions and additional research questions are presented as a basis for further research. We must learn how effectively to administer our information resources for improved decision making if we are to solve the various problems that will confront the academic library during the next decade. This volume can help provide some direction to other researchers who wish to examine organizational information handling.

My personal observations, as well as the numerous informal comments that do not appear in the data, suggest that a number of academic librarians will enter the 1980s without adequate administrative skills—especially in areas of decision making and planning—to confront the problems associated with effective resource allocation. By and large, library directors have not been formally trained in administrative skills, professional librarians have not had an effective opportunity to influence the direction of their library, and the importance of mechanisms to acquire, analyze, and disseminate information for decision making is only now being recognized.

Thus, the early 1980s must be a time of "catch-up" for library administration, especially compared to administrative strategies that have been used and developed for decades in the business world. For most academic libraries, the most probable method of increasing effectiveness will be improved administration through better information handling and decision making. Such an approach assumes better utilization of human resources as the principal means to improve overall library effectiveness.

This book is designed to be of interest primarily to academic librarians, although college and university administrators, researchers in organizational communication and information processing, and library educators should also be concerned with the issues addressed. Although the book reports basic research with analysis and practical strategies, the final chapter is especially intended to serve the practitioner as a guide to action. The final chapters include models of issues such as political impact of information, evaluation of information sources, and information-handling ability that are intended to be catalysts to stimulate questions for future research. And, finally, the book is intended to summarize recent thought, on an interdisciplinary basis, regarding information for decision making. Thus, both researchers and practitioners within and outside library and information science will find areas of interest in the volume.

Acknowledgments are many to those who assisted in the development of this book. Initial interest in this topic was encouraged by Drs. Ernest R. DeProspo, Ralph Blasingame, and Susan Artandi of Rutgers University, Graduate School of Library and Information Service. Their original direction of the doctoral dissertation laid the groundwork on which I could continue the research at the University of Oklahoma.

Thanks are also in order to the College of Arts and Sciences at the University of Oklahoma, which provided a faculty research grant during 1978 to continue the project and concentrate on the evaluation of information sources for decision making. Without their support a critical component of the research could not have been addressed.

I am also indebted to Dr. James S. Healey, Director of the School of Library Science at the University of Oklahoma, for his encouragement, counsel, and moral support of the project. His concern and initial suggestions provided the impetus to continue my research in this area. Moreover, his confidence in the overall value of the project contributed to its completion.

To the numerous academic librarians who participated in the two studies, a special note of gratitude is made. Researchers often forget that without their cooperation there can be no data, no analysis, and no recommendations for change. The high response rate and overall interest in the project among those who participated in the data collection is, perhaps, indicative of their concern for the topic. Their assistance is greatly appreciated.

And, finally, a note of thanks is due to Susan Randall and Jackie Elliott for their assistance in typing the manuscript and revising various figures and sections as needed. The task of typing and arranging the final manuscript was efficiently done by them, for which I am especially grateful.

INFORMATION
FOR ACADEMIC LIBRARY
DECISION MAKING

1

INTRODUCTION

ORGANIZATIONAL INFORMATION HANDLING

Today's academic librarian is a decision maker regardless of his or her specific job title and position in the organization. As a decision maker, the librarian can have a significant effect on the daily activities taking place in the library, the ongoing operations of the library, and the services that are provided to the patrons. Recognition of the professional librarian as a decision maker is a primary step toward improved decision making in the academic library.

Thus, the librarian is the single most important resource of the library organization. Money, materials, and equipment must be activated by the individual to accomplish a specific objective. People make decisions. As the library's most important resource the librarian is assumed to be knowledgeable about various library-related matters, such as buying material, providing information services, cataloging and classifying, and numerous other tasks. But what about all the administrative aspects of the librarian's job? What tasks are to be accomplished here?

Many librarians take their first position only to learn in short order that, by default, they are now decision makers because of their professional status. As a professional librarian, the clerical help, student assistants, patrons, and other librarians assume that the librarian is knowledgeable about scheduling, budgeting, personnel matters, security systems, and other matters. Frequently, the librarian is forced into decision making if for no other reason than that he or she is there.

Typically, the title of decision maker has been arbitrarily ascribed only to directors and assistant or associate directors. Psychologically this suggests that only administrators make decisions and that librarians need not be involved in the decision-making process. When most decisions are forced up the hierarchy for resolution, a substantial portion of the human resources in the library is wasted.

With the milieu of social, economic, political, and psychological factors affecting the various decisions that are made, the decision maker's task of reaching rational decisions becomes increasingly difficult. Regardless of its complex nature, important decision making is an everyday occurrence. Yet very little is known about (1) what factual information sources librarians in an academic library contact during organizational decision making, (2) the frequency or number of such contacts, (3) which organizational members provide informational input into the library decision-making process, and (4) which information sources are preferred for what types of decisions.

The complexity of the typical academic library, the broad range of decisions that must be made, and the need to obtain maximum benefits from limited resources demand a rational approach to decision making. If people are the most important resource in the library, then a rational approach is to obtain everyone's full potential of productivity. Each person must be able to carefully examine the various situations he or she faces, and make "rational" decisions.

The most significant aspect of the decision-making process is the individual's use of information sources as a basis for the decision. Of course, one assumes that all decisions are based to some degree on informational input; but the meaning of the word "information" in that assumption may have to be heavily qualified. In a formal organization such as the academic library, the relationship between information sources and decision making is crucial for improving the decision-making process.

Despite the importance of information sources, a decision maker rarely thinks about the specific information sources utilized to make a decision nor does the decision maker consider specific steps taken in the decision-making process. What information sources are librarians contacting to make organizational decisions? Why are some sources selected and others ignored? What strategies can librarians utilize to improve their informational input for the decision-making process?

These questions must be raised in order to utilize better the human resources in the library. The successful operation of an academic library depends on many factors, but one of the most important is the ability of the organization to change, initiate, and respond to various environmental factors. To do this, the organizational members accumulate information pertaining to the situation, analyze it, and reach some decision. The success of the decision, and thus the effectiveness of the organization, will be closely related to the quality of the information used to make the decision as well as the decision-making process used by the organization.

Regardless of formal position in the organization, the librarian is an information processor—not only in the provision of services to the patrons but also as a decision maker in the operation of the library. It is this second role of information processor to which attention must be drawn, for it is in this role that the librarian affects the decisions being made in the organization. Furthermore, it is with this role of organizational information processing that organizational members are least familiar and competent.

One of the basic topics addressed in this book was suggested by T. J. Allen in the late-1960s. Allen demonstrated that within a research and development organization certain people tend to have more contacts with selected types of factual information related to their profession. Additionally, Allen pointed out management's inability to recognize the existence of "information-rich employees," to understand the important role they play in the organization, or to exploit their special information-handling abilities for the benefit of the organization.

> Recognition and reward for performance as transmitters of information will ensure that gatekeepers continue in that capacity. Management presently appears either to discourage this activity by failing to reward it, or to reward the gatekeeper by promotion and thereby make it impossible for him to continue as a transmitter of information [within the organization] .[1]

Since that time (1969) limited field research has addressed this topic or studied the role of information-related variables in the organization as a whole or, more specifically, in the decision-making process.

All organizational members in an academic library operate as transmitters of information—some better than others. They must have access to and analyze information as input in the decision-making process and become "organizational information conscious" if they hope to improve the decision-making process and, thus, the ability of the library to make decisions that accurately reflect the needs of the environment. All organizational members have the potential to improve their information-handling ability to resolve library decision situations. The ability of the librarian to acquire, analyze, and disseminate information related to organizational decision making is as important as the ability to acquire, analyze, and disseminate information for the library patron, and it is to the former topic that this book is directed.

The societal context in which the librarian exists is composed of two equally important parts. The first has been described by Peter F. Drucker. He writes that perhaps the greatest challenge facing today's manager is putting ideas to work, that is, making knowledge productive. The basic resource from which the administrator must draw is the knowledge worker, "who puts to work what he has learned in systematic education, that is concepts, ideas, and theories, rather than the man who puts to work manual skill or muscle."[2] To manage this emerging type of worker effectively, administrators are becoming increasingly concerned with understanding the process by which information is transferred within an organization. Only through such understanding can the administrator hope to develop the full potential of these workers who must daily communicate to others in an organization information from which decisions are made, programs and operations are operated, and goals are set.

In addition to recognizing the existence of the knowledge worker, the concept of the post-industrial society is also an important context. According to Daniel Bell, the United States is well along in the process of becoming a post-industrial society, that is, one based largely on an economy of services rather than on an economy of goods-producing industries.[3] He identifies categories of service-producing industries, some of which are health, education, research, and government. In terms of organization, functions, and skills, he notes the similarities among these service-producing industries. For effective productivity these service-oriented industries must recognize critical aspects of the Knowledge Society and learn, as Peter Drucker has suggested, how to put knowledge to work. Both Bell and Drucker believe that the future success of the United States is dependent on our administrative ability to operate service-oriented industries within the setting of the Knowledge Society.

Our administrative ability to operate service-oriented industries such as the library will depend to no small degree upon our ability to marshal various information resources to resolve complex decision situations. Indeed, the future success of the academic library may well depend on the librarian's ability to recognize him- or herself as a knowledge worker in the post-industrial society rather than as a white collar worker in the industrial society.

The administrative philosophy that seems best suited to leading the librarian's organizational information-handling capacity has been termed "contingency management." This relatively new school of management thought emphasizes the importance of environmental factors in developing effective managerial strategies. Writers such as Harold Koontz,[4] Fremont E. Kast,[5] and Fred Luthans[6] suggest that individuals are more likely to modify organizational behavior by manipulating environmental characteristics than to make direct threats and promises to other individuals in the organization. In short, these writers suggest that manipulating environmental factors is more effective than attempting to manipulate personal behavior. The manipulation and control of organizational information acquisition and dissemination appears to be a preliminary "environment" that must be examined as a prerequisite for improved decision making and organizational effectiveness. Based on contingency management notions, librarians can learn how to manipulate *their* information environment and understand the complex nature of organizational information handling.

Organizational information handling is the process by which organizational members efficiently and effectively acquire, organize, and disseminate information related to the operation of the library for improved decision making. This task is the responsibility of all organizational members but especially the professional librarian. The context in which this task takes place is the library as a post-industrial organization in which the members are basically knowledge workers. The managerial philosophy that appears to be best suited to understanding and improving organizational information handling is the contingency approach. Based on these tenets the relationship between information sources and decision making can be exploited to increase the effectiveness of the academic library organization.

INFORMATION SOURCES

The term "information" can be defined as data of value for decision making; information must have the potential to reduce, resolve, or increase the uncertainty of a person vis-à-vis a specific situation.[7] Numerous types of information have been suggested by researchers based on criteria such as source, mode of transmission, or utilization—each of which implies a different level of analysis. Regardless of the criteria, any type of information must have the *potential* to change the certainty-uncertainty state of an individual.

At an organizational level of analysis employees obtain information from numerous sources which they, in turn, may use to perform duties required by their position in the organization. The range of possible information sources that may help the employee perform his or her job is vast. However, with certain types of professional employees—such as academic librarians—a selected number of possible information sources may be suggested as indicators of their contact with information that they find useful in the performance of the job and as input to the decision-making process.

One must not confuse an information source with meaning. C. K. Ogden and I. A. Richards point out that the meaning of a symbol or word involves the relationship of the symbol to the transmitter, the receiver, and the symbol itself. Only messages are transmittable and meanings are not in the message but in the message users.[8] In fact, two messages or information sources, one with meaning and one which is meaningless, could be exactly equivalent in information, or number of bits transmitted.[9]

For purposes of this study, a selected number of information sources will be referred to as "factual." The term factual does not imply accuracy or value, nor does it ignore the consideration that factual information inevitably will be filtered through the receiver's cognition processes. Because of the difficulties involved in defining information in general and factual information in particular, specific kinds of information sources typically utilized by librarians for organizational decision making will be defined as factual sources of information.

Examples of factual information sources are professional meetings, committee meetings, journals, books, interpersonal contacts, telephone calls, and memos. Identification and description of the factual information sources, or situations that are indicative of a factual information source, to be used throughout this study will be detailed in the various chapters as needed. The factual information sources are used as vehicles by which one can count the number of times the librarian comes into contact with a given source or to describe information sources that are used as input for decision situations. The total number of contacts with factual information sources is an indicator of the relative amount of factual information acquired by that librarian related to various decision situations.

In their studies of information flow in research and development organizations, T. J. Allen,[10] William J. Paisley,[11] and Winford E. Holland[12] have found that certain people tend to come into contact with "more" and "better" sources of information in the performance of their job. Such people might be called organizational information rich.

Some of the characteristics of organizational information-rich are: they read more articles and reports; they publish more monographs, articles, and reports; they have more interpersonal contacts with other professionals both within and outside the organization; and they are recognized by their colleagues as more likely to help solve research problems. Additionally, the information rich tend to receive more respect, to have higher status, and to be more "positive" toward their job and the organization as a whole. Thus, an organizational information-rich employee can be defined as one who comes into contact with more sources of factual information related to his or her position, profession, or organization than other employees in the same organization.

However, it must be recognized that because they come into contact with more sources of factual information than other organizational members does not mean that the information held by such people is relevant to the organizations' goals or management's information needs or that the information selected for acquisition by one person is appropriate or "best" for another individual.

Increased contact with organizational information sources by library staff may contribute to the likelihood of their being involved in the decision-making process, to the overall effectiveness of the final decision, and to the ability of the individual to select and utilize certain information sources for specific decision situations. Ultimately, increased awareness of one's organizational information-handling ability will provide a framework in which to improve the effectiveness of one's decisions.

The limited research pertaining to this notion of information rich employees and organizational information handling has concentrated on research and development sections within a larger organization and has not examined the information-handling abilities of either an administrator or a librarian in the decision-making process. However, such concepts may help librarians to better understand the relationship between information sources and decision making in organizations such as an academic library.

DECISION MAKING

Decision making is an integral part of the management and effective operation of any organization. In recent years many academic libraries have grown into multimillion-dollar organizations where librarians daily make decisions on a myriad of complex problems involving relatively large amounts of money, relatively large numbers of staff, and with numerous results affecting the library patron for good or ill.

The study of decision making usually involves three related topics: the decision-making process, the decision maker, and the decision itself. Within each of these topics, decision making aims to influence value judgments. But if one defines decision making as that process whereby information is converted into action, then decision making is largely concerned with the process of acquiring, controlling, and utilizing information to accomplish some objective.[13]

During the decision-making process the decision maker not only needs the ability to ask the right questions and judge the right answers but also to gather and assess the information relevant to a particular decision. Thus, a major task for the decision maker is to identify what information is needed to serve as a basis for making the decision, to determine the means by which the information can be made available to the decision maker, and decide when enough information has been obtained on which to base a decision.

Herbert Simon has pointed out the schizophrenia of researchers who have studied the decision-making process. At one extreme, economists attribute to man an omniscient rationality: he is aware of all information and alterations pertaining to a decision situation and there are no limits to the complexity of the computations he will perform to determine which alternatives are best. At the other extreme are those who tend toward social psychology, reducing all decision making to cognition and affect. Simon introduces the concept of bounded rationality and suggests two criteria for rational decision making: (1) a goal must be established as to the preferred outcome from the decision, and (2) the elected action must be a choice among two or more alternatives.[14]

Simon also suggests that, although economic man maximizes or selects the best from among all alternatives available, administrative man "satis-fices," or looks for a course of action that is satisfactory or "good enough."[15] The concept of administrative man is a logical extension of Simon's notion of bounded rationality: administrative man identifies al-ternatives and information that will provide for a satisfactory decision, not the best possible one. Simon suggests that the decision-making pro-cess is described more realistically in terms of his concepts of bounded rationality, administrative man, and satisficing.

This study draws upon Simon's notions of administrative man and satisficing to describe the decision-making process in an academic library organization. Because of the concept of bounded rationality, the decision maker frequently must rely on the expertise of other organizational mem-bers either to provide him with the actual information needed or to direct him to the proper sources where the information can be obtained. The wide range of problems and complex nature of the academic library or-ganization force the administrator's dependence on information from other individuals and make it less likely that decisions will be made uni-laterally.

At an organizational level of analysis some researchers regard the in-dividuals *and* the organization as information-gathering and information-processing systems. Such a framework of analysis suggests that to remain vital the organization must exchange information and other resources with its environment by receiving, transmitting, and disseminating infor-mation. Decision making based on an open systems framework stresses the interdependence of all organizational members on both each other and the factual information sources inside and outside the organization.[16]

The quantity of factual information required to make a decision de-pends on the situation, the time element, the quality of the information sources, the cost to obtain the information, and a host of other variables. But based on Simon's model of administrative man, the open systems model of an organization, and the complextiy of today's academic library, it may be suggested that all organizational members rely on other in-dividuals during the decision-making process because of their need for factual information sources as well as other standard social variables. The notion of an organizational information-rich employee is an im-portant concept that can be used to link the professional librarian's information-handling ability with information sources and organizational decision making.

INFORMATION FOR DECISION MAKING

Information for decision making is clearly concerned with two major concepts: (1) information, and (2) decision making. But it must be recognized that these concepts as used in this study have been given limited and specific definitions. Indeed, a major problem for researchers in this field is to restrict the number of variables and define critical terms to make the study manageable without losing a true representation of either "information" or "decision making."

The relationship between information and decision making is crucial and is further complicated because a decision maker is likely to have a different "decision state" from another decision maker relative to a given decision situation. Each decision maker has a different base of information, experiences, and opinion. Decision makers do not come into a decision situation with a clean slate that can be easily compared to another decision maker's.

Despite these complications, the decision maker, as a result of complex personal characteristics, various environmental factors, his or her decision state, and the number of sources of factual information contacted, can produce some decision. That decision is a choice in an ongoing process of evaluating various alternatives. The selected action or actions is purposeful, that is, intended to accomplish a desired goal.

One group of administrators might contend that although it is necessary to obtain factual information and evaluate alternatives, it is more important that the "good" decision maker use wise judgment, have a feel for the problem, rely on common sense and past experiences, and be decisive.

Administrators from another school of thought might suggest that a "good" decision maker will seek out and accumulate all factual information that pertains to the decision situation by both collecting written documents and speaking to experts familiar with the problem. Based on this accumulation of information, the "good" administrator then objectively evaluates the various courses of action and chooses the best alternative to accomplish a given objective. A representation of these conflicting schools of thought relating factual information to decision making is presented in Figure 1-1.

The continuum represented in Figure 1-1 illustrates the quantity of factual information that might be acquired by two different decision makers. The term "born" decision maker might be applied to one who seems immediately to grasp (or believes he or she grasps) the nature of the decision situation without having to rely on numerous sources of information to make the decision. The other extreme is a decision maker, referred to as the "factual" decision maker, who actively seeks and accumulates large amounts of factual information from both written and interpersonal sources in order to make a decision.

Contingency management theory would suggest that neither method is in itself "good," but each depends on a host of variables related to the information sources and the decision situation. However, it can be suggested that there is a positive relationship between contacting relevant information sources and the quality of the decision—at least until information overload occurs. In a complex organization the decision maker frequently may combine both techniques depending on the nature of the decision situation and its likely outcomes.

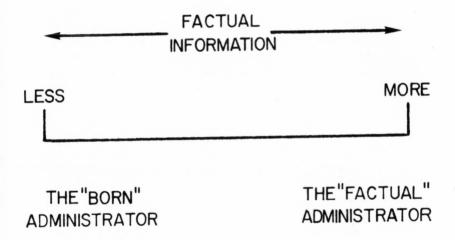

FIGURE 1-1   Information for Decision Making

THE NATURE OF THE STUDY

Research related to organizational information handling and decision making must (1) devise a means to describe and quantify factual information sources that may be used in organizational decision making, and (2) analyze the various types of information sources used for typical library decision situations. Based on such research, strategies can be suggested to improve organizational information management in the academic library.

Answers to the following questions would help librarians to better understand their information handling characteristics and their involvement in the library decision-making process.

1. Do library administrators come into contact with more or fewer sources of factual information than other professionals in the academic library?
2. What is the number of contacts with factual information sources for different kinds of professional librarians within a "typical" academic library?
3. Whom do librarians rely upon for information within the library as input for organizational decision making?
4. What are the social and educational characteristics of academic library organizational information rich compared to other members in the organization?
5. What information sources are perceived to be most valuable for the resolution of typical library decisions?
6. What information seeking networks exist in a typical library and how can they be exploited for improved decision making?
7. Can library decisions be categorized by the kind of information utilized in its resolution?
8. What managerial strategies can be utilized to increase the information-handling ability of the librarians for more effective decision making?

With a better understanding of organizational information handling in the library organization, academic librarians can assess their role and the role of others in the decision-making process and organize their information-handling activities to improve organizational decision-making effectiveness.

Throughout this chapter definitions, assumptions, and limitations of the study have been suggested. However, specific attention should be drawn to additional parameters affecting the study. The terms "information," "decision making," "information sources," and "organizational information handling" have already been defined. But the terms "library administrators" and "librarians" have not been clearly distinguished.

In this study the term administrator is used to describe a person in the academic library who (a) has overall responsibility for library operations (usually referred to as the director), or (b) has been previously designated to act in the director's place in his or her absence (usually referred to as assistant or associate directors).

The term "librarian" is meant to include all other professional employees in the library. Typically the librarian has received a master's degree in library/information science or some related discipline. Both librarians and administrators may be involved in the decision-making process, but each may have a different perspective on organizational information and use of information for decision making.

The research conducted in this study assumes that library decision makers may obtain or contact factual information from other members in the organization, from people outside the organization, and from an infinite possible number of written sources. Regardless of the information sources, organizational members do not work in isolation from information related to the operation of the library or to their specific job responsibilities.

Also, it is assumed that the decisions made in an academic library are based to some degree on the factual information (regardless of source) with which organizational members have contacted. Recognizing that such information is likely to be filtered through a myriad of internal perceptual processes, it nonetheless serves as a basis for decisions or as input to the decision-making process.

Although it is recognized that certain information sources may have more or less impact on the resolution of a given decision situation, the degree of that impact on an interval scale of measurement cannot, at this time, be determined. Therefore this study assumes that all sources of organizational information have the same *potential* to be of value for a given decision situation. Individual preferences for one source over another may suggest perceived value but the measure of that value is understandable only in relation to other sources that have impact on that decision.

In order to define a topic that is both manageable and feasible, yet useful to the profession, a number of limitations have been imposed on the study. First, organizational members' sources of information will be examined largely within the context of the position, profession, and organization with which they work. The myriad outside sources such as the home, family, and church will not be examined as to their relation either to information acquisition or the decision-making process within the library.

This study will not identify or describe personality characteristics or personal intelligence, although it can be assumed that both factors may affect to some degree the information acquisition characteristics and activity of the individual during the decision-making process. The emphasis of this study is on the number and kind of factual information sources organizational members contact, perceived value of those sources, and the persons' corresponding involvement in the decision-making process— not individual personality characteristics.

Also, it is recognized that the library administrator as well as the individual librarian may be affected by the organizational structure and his or her relative position within that structure in terms of information acquisition and decision making. However, although the relationship of status or organizational title to information-handling ability will be discussed, the degree to which the formal structure affects the decision-making process and the individual's contact with information will not be formally studied.

Primarily, the intent of this work is to present the author's research findings and integrate those findings with other studies concerning organization informational handling and decision making. Through such a method an interdisciplinary approach to the study of information for decision making can be accomplished.

The second purpose of the work is to provide a framework of analysis by which an individual organizational member in the academic library can examine his or her information-handling ability and corresponding involvement in decision making. Academic librarians must become more conscious of the sources of information they utilize as input to decision making. This work should suggest methods of individual as well as organizational information-handling self-analysis.

Finally, this book intends to assist librarians improve both the effectiveness and efficiency of academic library decision making. Effective decision making is the accomplishment of predetermined objectives as a result of the decision made. Efficient decision making is the resolution of the decision situation in reduced time or with reduced cost. These are important distinctions to recognize. Improved decision making will have payoffs not only for the organization but also for its patrons. Furthermore, increasing the effectiveness and efficiency of organizational decision making provides an opportunity for organizational members to develop their full potential as productive members in that organization. Developing strategies for improved organizational information management appears to be one method to improve organizational effectiveness.

The findings that will be presented in this study are based on data collected from academic librarians in medium-sized libraries from both the northeastern and the southwestern United States. Because of the similarity of responses, information sources available to professional librarians regardless of their geographic location, and typical decisions that face all library organizations, the results may be tentatively generalized to a number of academic libraries meeting certain criteria. Additionally, the results will allow academic librarians to compare their situation to that presented in this study.

The results of the research presented in this study are tentative because of the exploratory research approach taken with the topic. Similar studies in the social sciences are few and studies dealing with this topic in the academic library setting are nonexistent. Nonetheless, the combination of these results and related research may provide a catalyst for future research and for academic library decision makers to carefully examine their information-handling activity in the library decision-making process.

NOTES

1. T. J. Allen and S. I. Cohen, "Information Flow in Research and Development Laboratories," *Administrative Science Quarterly,* 14 (March 1969): 19.

2. Peter F. Drucker, *Management: Tasks, Responsibilities, Practices* (New York: Harper & Row, 1973), p. 32.

3. Daniel Bell, *The Coming of Post Industrial Society* (New York: Basic Books, 1973).

4. Harold Koontz and Cyril O'Donnell, *Management: A Systems and Contingency Analysis of Managerial Functions,* 6th ed. (New York: McGraw-Hill, 1976).

5. Fremont E. Kast and James E. Rosenzweig, *Organization and Management: A Systems Approach,* 2nd ed. (New York: McGraw-Hill, 1974).

6. Fred Luthans, *Introduction to Management: A Contingency Approach* (New York: McGraw-Hill, 1976).

7. This definition is expanded from Bruce J. Whittemore and M. C. Yovits, "A Generalized Conceptual Development for the Analysis and Flow of Information," *Journal of the American Society for Information Science,* 24 (May-June 1973): 222.

8. C. K. Ogden and I. A. Richards, *The Meaning of Meaning* (London: Routledge & Kegan Paul, 1949).

9. Susan Artandi, "Information Concepts and Their Utility," *Journal of the American Society for Information Science,* 24 (July-August 1973): 242-45.

10. Allen, "Information Flow in Research and Development Laboratories," 12-14.

11. William J. Paisley, "Information Needs and Uses," in *Annual Review of Information Science and Technology,* vol. 3, ed. Carlos A. Cuadra (Chicago: Enclyclopaedia Britannica, 1968), pp. 1-30.

12. Winford E. Holland, "The Special Communicator and His Behavior in Research Organizations: A Key to the Management of Informal Technical Information Flow," *IEEE Transactions on Professional Communication*, PC-17 (September-December 1974): 48-53.

13. Colin Eden and John Harris, *Management Decision and Decision Analysis* (New York: John Wiley & Sons, 1975), p. 57.

14. Herbert Simon, *Administrative Behavior,* 3rd ed. (New York: The Free Press, 1976), pp. xxvi-xxxi.

15. Ibid., pp. xxvi-xxxi.

16. Kast and Rosenzweig, *Organization and Management.*

2

INFORMATION
FOR DECISION MAKING:
AN OVERVIEW

INTRODUCTION

The general research area with which this study is concerned can be labeled
information for decision making. Numerous disciplines within the social
and mathematical sciences are exploring this area, often with different
assumptions, definitions, and methodologies. However, the overall purpose
of much of this research is to better understand and improve the decision-
making process. But the interdisciplinary interest, the relative newness of
the field, and the difficulty in defining many of its critical terms make this
field complex and at times contradictory.

Since it is known that the typical organizational employee spends approximately 70 percent of the working day communicating with fellow
workers,[1] the sources of the information, the use made of various information channels, and the specific patterns of communication interaction
among the employees take on added significance. Also of critical importance for the organizational decision maker is the role that the individuals
play in the process of acquiring, processing, and utilizing the various information sources available to employees in the organization.

The study of organizational communication is itself frequently con-
founded because of a lack of agreement concerning adequate definitions
of such basic terms as communication. F. E. X. Dance reviewed ninety-
five definitions from the literature and was unable to amalgamate into a
cohesive definition the fifteen somewhat disparate themes which emerged.[2]
Lee O. Thayer has reached a similar conclusion after noting problems of

theory development in communication research.[3] Of equal importance, because of the emphasis of this review, is the confusion surrounding the notion of information richness.[4]

Within the field of organizational communication various methods of study from such diverse disciplines as social psychology, organization theory, information science, management science, cognitive psychology, and communication networks (to name a few) have been employed. Frequently, the shift from one discipline to another—although studying the same phenomenon—causes a jumble of different kinds of jargon, definitions, assumptions, and, inevitably, results.

Although the main topic of this review is information for decision making, three subject areas can be identified that pertain to the topic. The first is the notion of information richness. Information richness is that phenomenon by which certain individuals are better able to acquire, process, and utilize information than are other individuals in the organization. Within this context, such topics as information seeking, organizational communication, communication networks, and information use have presented discussions of factors that directly relate to understanding the acquisition, processing, and transfer of information within the organization as well as on an individual basis.

The second subject with which this review deals comes under the broad heading of decision making. Decision making may be defined as the conversion of information into action. Although numerous publications deal with the notion of decision making, only those that specifically address the relationship between information and decision making will be included in this review.

The third topic of interest to this review is the relationship between organizational information and management. Ultimately, the purpose of research related to information for decision making is to improve the organizational decision-making process. Effective strategies for improved organizational decision making have to consider various management styles as a means for implementing the strategies. Contingency management theory as it relates to management strategies and information will be briefly reviewed.

The purpose of the review is to bring together writings related to information richness, information for decision making, and the relationship between information and management. The review attempts to be interdisciplinary and emphasizes recent literature whenever possible, but it is selective rather than comprehensive and refers only to those works that (1) form the general basis for the topic, (2) deal specifically with the three topics of interest, and (3) provide a basis for speculation about the effect of information sources on organizational decision making.

INFORMATION RICHNESS

Clearly, most of the research that has been conducted on the notion of information richness has come from information use studies, largely in the research and development setting. Research by T. J. Allen,[5] William Paisley,[6] J. M. Brittain,[7] Diana Crane,[8] Anne Wilkin,[9] and Susan Crawford[10] frequently touches upon notions of information richness. Although research in the social sciences has investigated communication networks, few attempts have been made to describe this notion within the setting of an organization more oriented toward the traditional production of either services or material products. The notion of an employee as information rich has been little studied. Furthermore, those studies that have directly examined the concept employ different definitions and assumptions.

Perhaps the best overall empirical study of information use that deals specifically with the notion of information richness is one by Donald C. Pelz and Frank M. Andrews.[11] The population studied consisted of a group of scientists in a research organization, and one of the major findings of the study suggested a positive relationship between communication contacts and performance. This study is representative of other studies done in the social sciences in terms of specific settings and rather small populations. Nonetheless, the few studies that have been done either from the research and development setting or from traditional organizational settings suggest the importance of those individuals who can manage and utilize various information sources.

Largely from the research and development setting a number of communication studies by such writers as Eugene Jackson,[12] C. Glock and Herbert Menzel,[13] Menzel,[14] A. H. Rubenstein,[15] P. M. Hodge and G. H. Nelson,[16] T. J. Allen et al.,[17] Allen and S. I. Cohen,[18] Mauk Mulder and Henk Wilke,[19] J. W. Creighton et al.,[20] Winford E. Holland,[21, 22] Richard V. Farace and James A. Danowski,[23] Karlene H. Roberts and Charles A. O'Reilly,[24] John A. Czepiel,[25] and Charles R. McClure[26] study the information rich—although they do not necessarily refer to it by the same name. Thus, a number of comparisons can be made and are summarized in Table 2-1, Studies That Describe the Information Rich. In ad-

TABLE 2-1

Studies that Describe the Information Rich

SOURCE	NAME	FUNCTION	PERSONAL
Jackson (1951)	Liaison Person	Significantly influences and controls intergroup communications	
Glock and Menzel (1958)	Great Man	Receiver and transmitter of outside information	High status, relative higher rank
Menzel (1964)	Scientific Troubadour	Carrier of select information (know-how)	"No specific traits"
Hodge and Nelson (1965)	Information Specialist	Brings items of current interest to the attention of the group; relays intrafirm information	
Allen et al. (1968)	Internal Consultant	Answers technical questions for the group, given information about projects in process	High technical competence
Allen et al. (1968)	High Performer	High productivity in research; source of most external information via informal channels	Exceptionally high job performance
Allen and Cohen (1968)	Technological Gatekeeper	Source of outside information, more outside contacts, internal consultant on technical matters	Most patents, most papers published

Mulder and Wilke (1970)	Group Expert	Influences and to some degree controls participatory decision making	Greater availability of relevant information
Creighton et al. (1972)	Linker	Gathers, processes, distributes information; innovator and early knower of information	Innovator and opinion leader
Holland (1972, 1974)	Special Communicator	Seen by colleagues as the most valuable source of information in that organization or group	Greater exposure to information sources
Farace and Danowski (1973)	Liaison	More likely than others in the organization to serve as first source of information	High status and longer organization employment
Roberts and O'Reilley (1975)	"Expert"	Communicates information about specific tasks and knows where to obtain relevant information	High performance and greater organizational commitment
Czepiel (1975)	Early Adopter	Serves as source for information seekers through informal communication channels and is an opinion leader in the industry/field	Friendly, frequent and significant informal contacts
McClure (1977)	Organizational Information Rich	Influences organizational decision making, serves as informal opinion leader	High status, greater contact with information sources, involved in decision making

Source: Adapted from Winford E. Holland, "Information Potential: A Concept of the Importance of Information Sources in a Research and Development Environment," *Journal of Communication*, 22 (1972): 160.

dition, Farace and Danowski have summarized a number of communication studies from a more traditional organizational setting and also investigated this notion of information richness. Table 2-2, Summary of "Liaison Person" Attributes, summarizes these studies and describes the characteristics of "liaisons" within the formal organization.

Despite the different names and settings, all of these researchers either explicitly or implicitly write that the information rich is a carrier of select information who (1) answers questions of other people in the organization either directly or by indicating where the proper information source can be located, (2) demonstrates outstanding performance, (3) has greater exposure to information sources and interpersonal contacts, and (4) is frequently of higher status in the organization both formally and informally.

In terms of specific information acquisition characteristics, the studies in Table 2-1 indicate that an information-rich employee reads more books, journal articles, and reports; publishes more articles, books, and reports; comes into contact with a large number of other professionals; and attends more conferences and meetings. Also of interest is that the information rich tend to have more interpersonal contacts with other members of the organization as well as professionals outside the immediate organization.

Because of the importance of interpersonal contacts a brief review of the communication network literature is helpful to further understand the information-handling characteristics of the information rich. Communication networks, and thus participants in those networks, are also affected by the nature and selection of communication channels and information sources. Perhaps the best treatment of this topic has been done by P. C. Gerstberger and T. J. Allen, who investigated various information channels as sources of information in a research and development environment.[27]

They found a direct relationship between perceived accessibility of the channel and its utilization—regardless of its quality. Although the study identified eight channels, similar studies have analyzed organizational communication through four basic channels: (1) face to face, (2) telephone, (3) reading, and (4) writing.[28] In general, interpersonal sources are more effective, people will choose the source that is most accessible, and little direct concern for the quality (accurateness) is actually considered. Despite these generalities, specific relationships

TABLE 2-2

Summary of "Liaison Person" Attributes

ACTUAL

1. Liaisons have higher agreement (between themselves and others they talk with) about whom their contacts are with than do nonliaisons.
2. Liaisons are more likely than others in the organization to serve as first sources of information.
3. Liaisons have higher formal status in the organization than do nonliaisons.
4. Liaisons have been organizational members for longer periods of time than have nonliaisons.
5. The levels of formal education and the ages of liaisons are similar to those of nonliaisons.

LIAISONS' PERCEPTION OF THEMSELVES

1. Liaisons perceive themselves to have greater numbers of communication contacts in the organization.
2. Liaisons perceive themselves to have greater amounts of information with respect to the content dimensions upon which their role is defined.
3. Liaisons perceive the communication systems as more "open"—information is seen as more timely, more believable, more useful, and so on.
4. Liaisons perceive themselves to have greater influence in the organization.

OTHERS' PERCEPTIONS OF LIAISONS

1. Liaisons are perceived by others to have greater numbers of communication contacts in the organization.
2. Liaisons' communication contacts are seen as having a wider range throughout the organizational structure.
3. Liaisons are perceived as having more control over the flow of information in the organization.
4. Liaisons are perceived as having more information on the content dimensions on which the network (or group) is defined.
5. Liaisons are perceived to have more influence over the "power structure" of the organization.
6. Liaisons are perceived to be more competent at their organizational activities.

Source: Adopted from Richard V. Farace and James A. Danowski, *Analyzing Human Communication Networks in Organizations: Applications to Management Problems* (East Lansing, Mich.: Michigan State University, Department of Communications, 1973), ERIC Document no. 099943, pp. 12-13.

between type of source, type of channel, actual situation, and type of use made of the channel are not well known.

Much research concerning communication networks centers on a breakdown between formal organization lines and the informal ones. Again, such research contributes to identifying specific *types* of information processors in the organization. An early researcher to examine this kind of categorization as to type of information processed/transferred was Herbert Menzel.[29] This dichotomy between formal and informal is still much in favor as a means to differentiate among types of communication. A recent report by Russell L. Ackoff and associates provides a clear definition of these two types of communication:[30]

1. Formal—asymmetrical communication with a lack of spontaneity and limited or restricted feedback, usually unidirectional.
2. Informal—symmetrical communication encouraging spontaneity and feedback, usually bidirectional.

Although numerous authors have used this breakdown, its usefulness specifically to describe *types* of participants, *amount* of information transferred, and *purpose* of the communicator is limited.

Despite the generally accepted proposition that informal or interpersonal communication tends to be more efficient and accurate, decision makers tend to depend equally on both formal and informal sources of information. An empirical study of decision makers in a public service institution by Renata Tagliacozzo, Manfred Kochen, and William Everett indicates that "oral, person-to-person communication was used as often as written communication to convey information."[31] Since the characteristics of the information rich (see Table 2-1) suggest a dependence on interpersonal communication, one might hypothesize that information-rich employees tend to be decision makers.

Recently, communication researchers Roberts and O'Reilly identified three basic types of communication networks in an organization, which they differentiate on a basis of function.[32]

1. Social Network—communication that is nonwork oriented, about information of a personal nature.

2. Authority Network—communication that details the responsibility
   and authority relationships among the various members of the organization.
3. Expertise Network—communication about a specific task, such as
   "how-to-do-it" or "how-to-improve-it" or where to obtain relevant
   information about it; information of a technical nature.

Based on empirical data, they theorize that all communication in the organization can be identified and classified according to these three criteria
and subsequently, by establishing who communicates to whom about
what, the communication networks within an organization can be mapped.
Their identification of "leaders" or "stars" within the expertise network
is of special interest to this review, as their characteristics are quite similar
to those of the information rich described in previously mentioned studies.

Sociometric mapping of communication networks has proven to be a
useful research tool in the study of the information rich. A recent investigation by Cosette Nell Kies employed sociograms to describe communication
patterns of personal reliance, informal information reliance, perceived influence, and friendship reliance in a public library organization. In each of
the various sociograms "stars" were identified—that is, people to whom most
communication was directed. Typically, stars in one network were not identified as stars in another network. This finding corresponds with findings
from Roberts and O'Reilly. Furthermore, Kies concludes that "most staff
members perceive the same individuals in the organization as being influ-
ential with the administration."[33]

Specific personality characteristics of the information rich have not been
directly studied, although some conclusions can be made from the studies
listed in Table 2-1. Nonetheless, such traits as friendliness,[34] competition
and ambition of the disseminator,[35] match of the communicator and receiver as either similar/dissimilar,[36] and the individual's value system[37]
appear to be major variables according to the existing literature. A recent
study of information utilization and personality by Jerome B. Kernan and
Richard Mojena describes three basic personality types with different information-seeking behavior. They conclude that "people do seem to use different information search styles and these are associated with reasonably
unique personality types."[38]

Our knowledge of the measurement of different types and degree of channel use, the amount of information selected, personality characteristics related to a person's information use, information-seeking networks, and kind of specific information sources utilized by the information rich is still quite limited. In general, it appears that a unique information specialist, the information-rich employee, can be identified in the formal organization on the basis of number of information sources contacted, reliance on interpersonal contacts, use of extraorganizational sources, and ability to synthesize divergent types of information into meaningful patterns for both him- or herself and the organization as a whole.

INFORMATION AND DECISION MAKING

A second major orientation one might employ to review the notion of organizational information is the subject of decision making. Some subtle but important differences in the concept of decision making appear in the research and development community (scientific information) and the market-oriented segments of the economy. Derek de Solla Price points out that knowledge is *not* consensual and free outside the hard sciences. Policy makers are under entirely different pressures from researchers, and information in the soft sciences—especially politically relevant matters—is not amenable to the same processes of transfer or study.[39] He stresses this point by further noting that innovations in organizations occur most of the time because of social pressures and market opportunities rather than the availability of new information.

The use of information and information processing for decision making is a subject that has received considerable attention in the literature. Various disciplines such as management science, organization theory, information science, and social psychology have been used as points for departure. Unfortunately for this review, only rarely are the notions of organizational information considered in the context of organizational decision making.

Most writers agree that effective information processing, flow, and utilization are vital for any organization. James G. March and Herbert A. Simon have analyzed organizations on the theory that organizational members are complex information processors and organizations are basically large decision-making units. Their major thesis is that the foundation of the organization is the flow and *rational* application of information (knowledge) to problems confronting the organization.[40] This view stresses the importance of acquiring, processing, and disseminating information to improve rational decision making in order to meet organization goals.

Conversely, researchers in the area of utilization of knowledge such as Ronald G. Havelock note that organizations are much more than a unified collection of people. Members of an organization must work together; they are interdependent.[41] To produce this interdependency among members within the organization there must be communication concerning what the objectives are, the means by which they will be reached, and the availability of information about the subject or decision situation.

Richard S. Farr has introduced the "knowledge linker" who activates the interpersonal network of communication between a target audience and gatekeepers.[42] Such concepts probably originate from the ideas of Elihu Katz and Paul Lazerfeld about the two-step flow of communication suggested in the mid-1950s.[43] Although Havelock's research stresses utilization of scientific knowledge, his introduction of the concept of a "linking-pin" process of information utilization, whereby *some people* must make contact with an outside resource system to help in decision making, addresses the notion of the information rich. Havelock stresses that "linkage is not simply a two person interaction process however; the resource person, in turn, must have access to more remote and more expert resources than himself."[44]

On an individual basis, Alex Bavelas has shown that "leaders" tend to give more information, to ask for more information, and to take the lead in summing up or interpreting a situation.[45] Of special interest to this subject is research recently completed by Virginia Richmond demonstrating that "opinion leaders" consistently have more information on the topic of their leadership than do nonopinion leaders.[46] It can be recognized that the main questions facing the organization leaders and decision makers are (1) How do I obtain relevant information concerning a given situation? and (2) When have I collected enough information to be able to make a decision? Whether one takes a holistic view of information processing as an organization function (March and Simon) or an interdependent view of group processing information to achieve organization objectives (Havelock), effective decision making depends on successful answers to these two questions. Thus, the decision maker is perceived as an information seeker, collector, organizer, and utilizer who processes information as a tool for effective decision making.

Another view of the decision maker's contact with information has been developed by Irving L. Janis. This researcher draws upon a conflict model of information seeking for decision making. Furthermore, his focus is on conditions that promote openness to challenging information, especially during the preliminary stages of the decision-making process. Analysis of a number of empirical studies has discounted the selective exposure hypothesis that people generally seek messages with which they agree and avoid those with which they disagree. Instead, Janis suggests a contingency view according to which, under certain conflict conditions, people tend to select certain information.

Janis's conflict model for information preferences is presented in Table 2-3. There are four main patterns of coping, and based upon these patterns, the person's dominant information mode, information preferences, and level of interest in information are suggested. Janis stresses that a decision maker's coping pattern is likely to depend on the nature of the decision situation, and perhaps most important, his or her degree of commitment to a specific action. The model is an excellent stimulus to research in the area of information for decision making and provides a contingency viewpoint that may be appropriate in a number of different organizations.[47]

Throughout the decision-making process at least eight constraints can reduce the effectiveness of a decision in terms of its information content. Harold D. Lasswell points out that information may be:

1. overlooked or ignored
2. withheld or concealed
3. rejected as from a noncreditable source
4. unbelievable in terms of established frame of reference
5. over- or underemphasized to the point of misuse
6. communicated incomprehensibly (alien tongue, jargon)
7. erroneously reported in good faith
8. deliberately misrepresented.[48]

In a recent study of distortion of organization information O'Reilly found that (1) low trust in the receiver of a message results in significantly more suppression by senders of information, especially information that reflects unfavorably on the sender, and (2) the measure of information distortion is significantly and inversely associated with job satisfaction and individual group performance.[49]

TABLE 2-3

Janis's Conflict Model Applied to Information Preferences

COPING PATTERN	DOMINANT INFORMATION MODE	CHARACTERISTIC INFORMATION PREFERENCES	LEVEL OF INTEREST IN INFORMATION
A. Unconflicted adherence	Indifference	Nonselective exposure	Low
B. Unconflicted change	Indifference	Nonselective exposure	Low
C. Defensive avoidance			
C-1 Procrastination	Evasion	Passive interest in supportive information; avoidance of all challenging information	Low
C-2 Shifting	Evasion	Delegation of search and appraisal to others	Low
C-3 Bolstering	Selectivity	Selective exposure; search for supportive information and avoidance of discrepant information	Medium

(continued)

TABLE 2-3 continued

| D. Hypervigilance | Indiscriminate search | Active search for both supportive and nonsupportive information, with failure to discriminate between relevant and irrelevant, trustworthy and untrustworthy | Very high |
| E. Vigilance | Discriminating search with openmindedness | Active search for supportive and nonsupportive information, with careful evaluation for relevance and trustworthiness; preference for trustworthy nonsupportive information if threats are vague or ambiguous | High |

Source: Reprinted with permission of MacMillan Publishing Co., Inc. from Irving L. Janis and Leon Mann, *Decision Making* (New York: The Free Press, 1977), p. 206.

The idea of a psychological cost in asking fellow employees for additional information was noted by Allen and Cohen[50] and has been tested in a real world situation by Dudley H. Dewhirst as an "information sharing norm."[51] By examining the concept of decison making as closely aligned with information seeking, Dewhirst notes the importance of *perceived* information-sharing norms in an organization. The physical accessibility and cost of the information from a fellow worker (perhaps an information-rich employee) may be small, but if the psychological cost, in terms of lost status or reputation, of obtaining the information is too great, the decision maker may choose to ignore it.

Another area for concern is the amount of information a decision maker is able to process effectively. A number of writers believe that a successful decision maker is one who is able to acquire, process, and disseminate "more" information. In one experimental research study, Avner M. Porat provided evidence that supports the hypothesis that "more information will result in more accurate levels of goal setting and decision making."[52] Kenneth Boulding has written, "there is also a considerable relationship between the capacity of a decision maker to handle large quantities of information and his ability to widen his agenda."[53] This open systems concept is further clarified by Milton Roeach, who suggests that the more a decision maker is disposed toward seeking new alternatives and additional information—that is, more environmental input—the more open the decision-making process will be.[54]

Yet, it must be noted that should the pendulum swing so far in the direction of information seeking that the person's information-seeking nature overwhelms his capacity to organize and process the information, the result might be information overload. Alex Inkeles points out that for the decision maker, the sheer stockpiling of information on some general basis, merely on the assumption that it might someday be useful, is not too helpful when crises actually arise.[55]

Janis also has pointed out that the "hypervigilant" fail to discriminate between relevant and irrelevant information, which results in information overload.[56] More useful than having access to the myriad bits of information would be to have access to some person who could put the various important bits into some meaningful scheme. Clearly an optimal level of information seeking within a person's cognitive capacity to process the information is required. How to determine what that level might be is a considerable problem. However, as George A. Miller has noted, information overload can be as detrimental to the decision-making process as a lack of relevant information.[57]

An empirical study by Alfred G. Smith clearly demonstrated that the information sources utilized for decision making by the "organization man" and the "research man" in the same research institute differ substantially. The organization man depends more on formal methods of communication, writes and reads more memos, spurns committee and other group meetings, and is much more likely to ask other members of the organization for advice or more information concerning a given subject.

Although this study was done in a research center, similarities to other kinds of organizations such as universities, hospitals, and research and development firms are striking. Both types of decision makers must at the same time provide and control information relating to certain (but different) subject areas as well as provide for the administration of the organization. Smith concludes his analysis by writing, "if the center were controlled by organization men, they could stifle research. But if the center were controlled by research men, there might not be a center at all."[58]

A decision maker's acceptance of scientific recommendations or use of information does not always reflect a basis of rationality that management scientists might expect. Simply because the factual data are available and especially pertinent to a given decision situation does not automatically mean that the decision maker will utilize the information. Thus, C. West Churchman reminds the researcher or "technician" that there is evidence to show that managers may have perfect information available but not make correct decisions. As Churchman writes, "we do not yet understand how to describe a human decison."[59]

Within the broad topic of information for decision making, a body of literature has developed that mathematically describes the process of making a decision under various states of uncertainty and with various amounts of information. Introduced by John von Neumann,[60] game theory and, later, decision theory have presented theoretical formulations by which statistical measures can be applied to decision making in certain types of situations. Decision theory was refined from the more general game theory by Abraham Wald. He has stressed that statistical decision problems are formulated within a stochastic process in which an infinite or finite collection of change variables have a joint probability distribution.[61]

Thomas S. Ferguson, in a recent sophisticated treatment of statistical decision theory, distinguishes between game theory and decision theory by noting that in a two-person game the players are trying simultaneously to maximize their winnings (or minimize their losses), whereas in decision theory nature determines a state without any clearly defined objectives in mind.[62] In a more basic treatment of decision theory, B. W. Lindgren states that there are four basic ingredients of a decision problem:

1. a set of available actions
2. a set of admissible states of nature
3. a loss (or gain) associated with each combination of a state of nature and an action
4. the amount of data available about the states of nature.[63]

Different theorems have been developed to describe the decision problem under conditions in which the decision maker has no data (complete uncertainty) or some amount of data. A measure of the loss or gain of the decision is provided by the concept of utility—the relative desirability of the consequences of a given decision for a given decision maker. This body of literature describing decision problems in statistical probabilities is limited to well-defined and simplistic decison situations. Often the theorems assume a normal distribution of amount of information, states of nature, and decision consequences which are not amenable to exact measurement or to describing complex decisions in the real world.[64]

Thus, the creation of a research technique that adequately represents the information-decision process in an organizational setting has been a major stumbling block for researchers in this discipline. In an excellent overview of information processing and decision making in organizations, Terry Connolly notes that greater research emphasis on "diffuse" decision making also is needed rather than on decision events. In his view, many decision processes cover long periods of time, have indistinct endpoints, and cover several organizational levels. Connolly concludes that greater emphasis also is needed to treat information processing and decision making within a single framework rather than as separate phenomena. Furthermore, he suggests that the primary focus should be "on the individual embedded in a decision process by means of his communication links to other individuals."[65]

In summary, the type and amount of information used by a decision maker to make a decision in any given situation are not clear; indeed, how one can scientifically describe a decision is not clear. Perhaps the basic difficulty with research in this area is one succinctly described by Ackoff: "one cannot specify which information is required for decision making until an explanatory model of the decision process has been constructed."[66] In short, study of information within the context of actual decision situations is necessary. A review of the information for decision-making literature indicates that the decision-making process is closely related to the decision maker's information acquisition characteristics. Specifics of that relationship can only be surmised. Other notions of information richness, communication contacts, organization structure, and management style also may affect the degree to which the decision maker can provide both efficient and effective decisions in the social, political, and economic milieu of that organization.

INFORMATION AND MANAGEMENT

A third approach to the idea of organizational information is through the various literatures related to management. For our purposes here, management will be defined as a decision-making process of coordinating organizational and environmental resources toward the accomplishment of certain goals. Indeed, according to Walter M. Carlson, "the one central fact which will control the management of information in the 1980s is that information conserves other resources through better decisions."[67]

Historically, various management schools of thought have evolved, each having a different perspective on organizational information processing. The scientific management school does not accord a very significant role to either communication or organizational information, and conceives of both largely in terms of command and control. Information flow is determined largely by superiors, lateral and upward flow is limited, information typically is transferred in a written format, and "managing" information is not considered.

The human relations school of thought perceives organizational information flow as more important than does the scientific school. Upward communication is stressed and the importance of information seeking and communication networks is identified. Management works to understand the information needs of the members and encourages information communication and social information transferal.

The systems or contingency view assumes the existence of untapped member capabilities and *designs* information flow techniques to tap these resources. Typically, there is full disclosure of information related to the setting of a goal. The contingency view of management suggests the importance of general systems notions as a means of manipulating various environments so that individuals in an organization can increase their personal and professional effectiveness as information handlers. Information feedback loops for evaluation and modification of actions are stressed and information processing is seen as the main function of all organizations.[68]

The historical analysis of information-related variables in the organization suggests that management has become increasingly concerned about such variables. Due in part to increased production and distribution of information related to the organization's goals, greater emphasis is given in recent management theory to environmental information rather than to internal information, and provision of methods to encourage flow of accurate information among organizational members is stressed.

At the organizational level of analysis, Richard K. Allen believes that the nature and extent of success and health in an organization depend upon an effective linkage between that organization and the external environment. He writes that today's progressive and successful organizations tend to display similar characteristics concerning information acquisition and use, specifically: (1) readiness to seek high quality outside information, (2) effective internal communication networks, and (3) a willingness to share information among organization members.[69]

Only recently has information management been recognized as a separate managerial function. W. W. Horton appears to have coined the term "IRM"—Information Resources Management—to describe the technique. He suggests that information is an organizational resource as important to the achievement of management's goals as the human resources, financial resources, and physical resources of the organization. The overall purpose of information resources management is to determine how information resources can be harnessed more effectively and efficiently to meet the decision-making and problem-solving needs of today's professionals. Throughout Horton's discussion of information resources management is the general acknowledgment that management has not yet recognized the importance of organizational information handling as a means to improve decision making.[70]

The concept of information resources management should not be confused with that of a management information system. Although literature related to management information systems is not within the scope of this review, a clarification of the two concepts is needed. Typically, a management information system supplies predetermined sets of information to selected individuals in the organization to aid in decision making. Downward flow of edited organizational information is stressed. The emphasis of the management information system is to *centralize and control* certain information, which tends to increase the power base of those few individuals who have access to the system.[71]

Information resource management attempts to decentralize information access and flow to all organizational decision makers rather than a select few. Upward and lateral information flow of environmental information is stressed within the open system concepts of negative entropy, homeostasis, and feedback. Information dissemination among all organization members is designed to provide each individual with accurate, relevant, and timely information. If one assumes that each member is a decision maker, then organizational information must be made available at the individual level of analysis.

In a recent review of the organizational decision process the author noted that the literature on management information systems implies an orientation toward standardized reporting procedures. Such systems tend to reinforce traditional scientific managerial premises of hierarchy, control, and standardization. Little attention is paid to the *individual* information needs of organization members. The conclusion reached by Ronald J. Ebert is that "we face a significant need for individual tailor-made information to facilitate decisions, information that goes beyond the standardized."[72]

According to Rensis Likert, organizations can be described on a measured continuum in terms of certain variables. The compilation of the scores for each variable presents a description or profile of the organization into different systems or styles of management. The continuum developed by Likert ranges from system 1 to system 4T, which includes very authoritative management systems (system 1) at one end to more open systems or a contingency view of management (system 4T).[73]

Likert states that the capacity of the organization to function well depends mainly on the quality of its decision-making process and the accuracy of the information used. He also provides some discussion on the effect of information-related variables vis-à-vis management style.[74] In his measurement instrument attention is paid to communication direction and accuracy, but information acquisition, processing, and dissemination in terms of types, value, and management of information are not discussed.

However, based on the Likert scale and other discussions of management style, it appears that different information use characteristics can be attributed to different management styles. Organizations with multi-directional information flow through the hierarchy that is accepted with an open mind and tends to be accurate as opposed to incorrect or censured is positively correlated with high productivity. One of Likert's theses is that managers can change their styles and move an organization toward system 4T—the most productive of the systems.[75]

Information acquisition, processing, and dissemination in participative managerial styles have not received wide attention. Maurice Marchant suggests that a participative managerial style in an academic library setting encourages productivity and better performance, but the role of organizational information vis-à-vis participation is not explored.[76] In addition, a review of the literature on participation by Louis Kaplan also uncovers little research related to information flow in the participative organization.[77] However, in one recent study, researchers found that participation may not equalize the power between the information haves and the information have-nots. Recognizing that, initially, power is held by the administrators (experts) and less power is held by the organizational members (others), imposition of participatory management styles in an organization with unequal information contact among members is likely to result in *greater* differences of power between the two groups.[78]

Victor Vroom has found that managers use decision processes providing less opportunity for participation when they possess all the necessary information to generate high quality decisions than when they lack some needed information. Contrarily, if managers' subordinates did have significantly added information or the managers did not have sufficient information, a more participative decision process would be employed.[79] The implication of Vroom's research is that unless organization members contact sources of information appropriate to organizational decisions, they should not expect to be involved in the decision-making process.

Information flow among administrators and subordinate members in an organization appears to be quite different. Structural variables of the organization do not appear to affect the frequency of administrative communication, whereas measures of organizational size and shape do appear to predict frequency of subordinate communication. The greater amount of authority the greater the frequency of communication contacts. Administrative communication contact appeared to be both downward and lateral, whereas subordinate communication contact is largely lateral.[80] The net effect of these patterns suggests managerial communication strategies with limited upward information flow, feedback, and perhaps maintenance of "information-poor" subordinates.

In an excellent review article of acquisition and utilization of technical information by administrative agencies, Paul Sabatier suggests that administrative agencies devote a considerable portion of their resources to the acquisition of technical information but that this information is often utilized to legitimate rather than to influence policy decisions. He presents a listing of variables affecting both the acquisition and utilization of information by managers and stresses that policy decisions are not based solely on technical information; normative elements invariably enter the decision process.[81]

Pragmatically, little writing appears on specific strategies that can be employed by a manager to encourage effective organizational information handling. However, Joel Goldhar suggests that more attention should be paid to designing and controlling the informational environment in the organization. Although referring to information management for innovation in a research and development setting, he believes that managers should encourage:

1. easy access to information by individuals
2. free flow of information both in and out of the organization
3. rewards for sharing, seeking, and utilizing "new" information
4. rewards for risk taking
5. rewards for accepting and adapting to change
6. mobility and interpersonal contacts.

Furthermore, Goldhar suggests that managerial stances that encourage the above factors provide an information environment in which organizational members can increase their creativity and productivity.[82]

Information-processing behavior of managers in terms of accurate estimates of future events has been studied by John R. Adams and Lloyd A. Swanson. In their study, they found that (1) the accuracy of a manager's estimates is positively related to the amount of information sought and processed, (2) the level of managerial talent possessed by a manager is positively related to the amount of information sought and processed, and (3) a manager's perceived importance of accurate estimates is positively related to the amount of information sought and processed. Similar to Goldhar, these researchers also suggest that changing or manipulating the manager's information environment could ultimately lead to an increase in accurate decision making for the organization as a whole.[83]

Overall, many researchers suggest that the results from information/decision-making studies have had little impact on management strategies. Henry Mintzberg writes that, in his opinion, "managers work as they always have, seeking information by word of mouth and using non explicit decision making procedures."[84] Although his analysis may be accurate, the need for information resources management in the organization has largely been ignored by researchers.

A brief overview of selected sources relating information to management suggests that information-related variables such as information acquisition, processing, and dissemination are important correlates to organizational effectiveness, responsiveness to the environment, and quality of decisions. Of the various managerial schools of thought, only contingency management provides a well-developed framework to study organizational information processing. This framework appears to be best described by Likert's system 4T. Furthermore, management styles can be devised to exploit the information environment in an organization to improve the performance of the individuals as well as the organization.

SUMMARY

In an excellent state of the art review of communication in organizations, Lyman W. Porter and Karlene H. Roberts suggest that we still know very little about (1) how information comes into organizations, (2) how it is internally generated in organizations, (3) how it is disseminated, regardless of its origin, and (4) differences between internally and externally generated information. They stress the need for empirical research to study information-related variables in the organizational setting.[85]

Furthermore, the current status of theory and research in interpersonal communication is built on four paradigms: (1) the situational approach, (2) the developmental approach, (3) the law-governed approach, and (4) the rule-governed approach. Gerald Miller believes that the developmental approach, that communicators relate to one another as social roles rather than as persons and develop communication strategies intended to reduce uncertainty about each other's roles in a dynamic ongoing developmental fashion, has the greatest potential for communication researchers.[86] Investigation of communication activities in terms of organizational roles and responsibilities is still in its infancy.

The review of literature presented in this chapter essentially agrees with the analysis of Porter and Roberts as well as Miller. While the importance of information in the decision- making process is generally recognized, little research specifically relates Porter and Roberts's questions to the decision-making process, managing the information environment, exploiting the organizational information rich in the decision-making process, or studying organizational information flow as a means to increase the productivity and effectiveness of both the individual employee and the organization as a whole.

The relevant literatures from the areas of the information rich, information for decision making, and information and management indicate the importance of the person's ability to acquire, process, and disseminate information. A combination of these literatures provides some clues to the factors affecting the acquisition of information and the notion of information richness in relation to organizational decision making and information/communication roles of organizational members.

Studies that deal directly with the concept of information richness *and* decision making or management are scant; indeed, most of the sources that are available concerning this topic come from studies that address such phenomena only in passing. Nonetheless, the research areas of the information rich, information and decision making, and information and management in an organizational context are virtually untapped and represent a great potential for better understanding and improving the organizational decision-information process.

NOTES

1. E. T. Klemmer and F. W. Synder, "Measurement of Time Spent Communicating," *Journal of Communication,* 22 (June 1972): 142-58.

2. F. E. X. Dance, "The Concept of Communication," *Journal of Communication,* 20 (September 1970): 201-10.

3. Lee O. Thayer, "On Theory-Building in Communication: Some Conceptual Problems," *Journal of Communication,* 13 (December 1963): 217-35.

4. Winford E. Holland, "Information Potential: A Concept of the Importance of Information Sources in a Research and Development Environment," *Journal of Communication,* 22 (June 1972): 142-58.

5. T. J. Allen, "Information Needs and Uses," in *Annual Review of Information Science and Technology,* vol. 4, ed. Carlos A. Cuadra (Chicago: Encyclopaedia Britannica, 1969), pp. 1-29.

6. William J. Paisley, "Information Needs and Uses," in *Annual Review of Information Science and Technology,* vol. 3, ed. Carlos A. Cuadra (Chicago: Encyclopaedia Britannica, 1968), pp. 1-30.

7. J. M. Brittain, *Information and Its Users* (New York: John Wiley & Sons, 1970).

8. Diana Crane, "Information Needs and Uses," in *Annual Review of Information Science and Technology,* vol. 6, ed. Carlos A. Cuadra (Washington, D.C.: American Society for Information Science, 1971), pp. 3-39.

9. Anne Wilkin, "Personal Roles and Barriers in Information Transfer," in *Advances in Librarianship,* ed. Melvin J. Voigt and Michael H. Harris (New York: Academic Press, 1977), pp. 257-97.

10. Susan Crawford, "Information Needs and Uses," in *Annual Review of Information Science and Technology,* vol. 13, ed. Martha Williams (White Plains, N.Y.: Knowledge Industries, 1978), pp. 61-81.

11. Donald C. Pelz and Frank M. Andrews, *Scientists in Organizations: Productive Climates for Research and Development* (New York: John Wiley & Sons, 1966).

12. Eugene Jackson, "Communication Practices in Complex Organizations," *Journal of Social Issues,* 7, no. 3 (1951): 37.

13. C. Glock and Herbert Menzel, *The Flow of Information Among Scientists: Problems, Opportunities and Research Questions* (New York: Columbia University, Bureau of Applied Social Research, 1958).

14. Herbert Menzel, "The Information Needs of Current Scientific Research," *Library Quarterly,* 34 (January 1964): 4-19.

15. A. H. Rubenstein, "Timing and Form of Researcher Needs for Technical Information," *Journal of Chemical Documentation,* 2 (January 1962): 28-31.

16. D. M. Hodge and G. H. Nelson, *Biological Laboratories Communication* (Fort Detrick, Frederick, Md.: U. S. Army Biological Laboratories, Technical Information Division, 1965).

17. T. J. Allen, A. Gerstenfeld, and P. G. Gerstenfeld, *The Problem of Internal Consulting in Research and Development Organizations* (Washington, D.C.: National Science Foundation, Office of Science Information Service, July 1965).

18. T. J. Allen and S. I. Cohen, "Information Flow in Research and Development Laboratories," *Administrative Science Quarterly,* 14 (March 1969): 12-19.

19. Mauk Mulder and Henk Wilke, "Participation and Power Equilization," *Organizational Behavior & Human Performance,* 5 (September 1970): 430-48.

20. J. W. Creighton, J. A. Jolly, and S. A. Denning, *Enhancement of Research and Development Output Utilization Efficiencies: Linker Concept Methodology in the Technology Transfer Process* (Monterey, Calif.: U. S. Navy Postgraduate School, 1972).

21. Holland, "Information Potential," 159-73.

22. Winford E. Holland, "The Special Communicator and His Behavior in Research Organizations: A Key to the Management of Informal Technical Information Flow," *IEEE Transactions on Professional Communication,* vol. PC-17, (1974): 48-53.

23. Richard V. Farace and James A. Danowski, *Analyzing Human Networks in Organizations Applications to Management Problems* (East Lansing, Mich.: Department of Communication, Michigan State University, 1973), ERIC Document no. 099943.

24. Karlene H. Roberts and Charles A. O'Reilly, III, *Communication Roles in Organizations: Some Potential Antecedents and Consequences* (Berkeley: Institute of Industrial Relations, University of California, 1975), NTIS Document no. A013 676/2GA.

25. John A. Czepiel, "Patterns of Interorganizational Communications and the Diffusion of a Major Technological Innovation in a Competitive Industrial Community," *Academy of Management Journal,* 18 (March 1975): 6-24.

26. Charles R. McClure, *Academic Librarians' Contact with Information Sources and Library Decision Making* (Rutgers University Ph.D. diss., 1977).

27. P. G. Gerstberger and T. J. Allen, "Criteria Used by Research and Development Engineers in the Selection of an Information Source," *Journal of Applied Psychology,* 52 (August 1968): 272-79.

28. Klemmer and Synder, "Measurement of Time Spent Communicating," 148-52.

29. Glock and Menzel, *The Flow of Information Among Scientists;* and, more recently, Herbert Menzel, "Informal Communication in Science, Its Advantages and Its Formal Analogues," in *Toward a Theory of Librarianship,* ed. Conrad Rawski (Metuchen, N.J.: Scarecrow Press, 1973), pp. 403-14.

30. Russell L. Ackoff et al., *The SCATT Report: A Tentative Idealized Design of a National Scientific Communication and Technology Transfer System* (Philadelphia: The Wharton School, University of Pennsylvania, 1975), pp. 403-14.

31. Renata Tagliacozzo, Manfred Kochen, and William Everett, "The Use of Information by Decision Makers in Public Service Organizations," in *Communications for Decision Makers: Proceedings of the American Society for Information Science,* vol. 8, ed. Jeanne B. North (Westport, Conn.: Greenwood Press, 1971), pp. 53-57.

32. Karlene H. Roberts and Charles A. O'Reilly, III. "Measuring Organizational Communication," *Journal of Applied Psychology,* 59 (June 1974): 321-26; Karlene H. Roberts and Charles A. O'Reilly, III, "Organizational Theory and Organizational Communication: A Communication Failure?" *Human Relations,* 27 (May 1974): 501-24; Karlene H. Roberts and Charles A. O'Reilly, III, *Organizations as Communication Structures: An Empirical-Theoretical Approach* (Berkeley: Institute of Industrial Relations, University of California, 1975), NTIS Document no. AD-A013675/4GA.

33. Cosette Nell Kies, *Unofficial Relations, Personal Reliance, Informal Influence, Communications, and Library Staff: A Sociometric Investigation of Three Medium-Sized Public Libraries* (Columbia University Ph.D. diss., 1977), p. 128.

34. John Czepiel, "Word of Mouth Processes in the Diffusion of a Major Technological Innovation," *Journal of Marketing Research,* 11 (May 1974): 172-78.

35. Jeffrey Crawford and Gordon A. Healand, "Predecisional Process and Information Seeking in Social Influence," in *Proceedings of the Annual Convention of the American Psychological Association* (New York: American Psychological Association, 1971), pp. 161-62.

36. Selwyn W. Becker, "Personality and Effective Communication in the Organization," *Personnel Administration,* 23 (July-August 1964): 28-30.

37. Kenneth Starck, "Values and Information Sources Preferences," *Journal of Communication,* 23 (March 1973): 74-85.

38. Jerome B. Kernan and Richard Mojena, "Information Utilization and Personality," *Journal of Communication,* 23 (September 1973): 325.

39. Derek de Solla Price, "Some Aspects of 'World Brain' Notions," in *Information for Action,* ed. Manfred Kochen (New York: Academic Press, 1975), pp. 177-92.

40. James G. March and Herbert A. Simon, *Organizations* (New York: John Wiley & Sons, 1958).

41. Ronald G. Havelock, *Planning for Innovation through Dissemination and Utilization of Knowledge* (Ann Arbor, Mich.: Center for Research on Utilization of Scientific Knowledge, 1969), pp. 6-2 through 6-3.

42. Richard S. Farr, *Knowledge Linkers and the Flow of Education Information* (Stanford, Calif.: ERIC Clearinghouse on Educational Media and Technology, 1969), ERIC Document no. 032438.

43. Elihu Katz and Paul F. Lazarsfeld, *Personal Influences: The Part Played by People in the Flow of Mass Communications* (Glencoe, Ill.: The Free Press, 1955).

44. Ronald G. Havelock, "Research on the Utilization of Knowledge," in *Information for Action,* ed. Manfred Kochen (New York: Academic Press, 1975), p. 97.

45. Alex Bavelas, "Leadership: Man and Function," in *Readings in Managerial Psychology,* ed. Harold J. Leavitt and Louis R. Pondy (Chicago: University of Chicago Press, 1964), p. 201.

46. Virginia Richmond, "The Relationship Between Opinion Leadership and Information Acquisition," *Human Communication Research,* 4 (Fall 1977): 38-43.

47. Irving L. Janis and Leon Mann, *Decision Making* (New York: The Free Press, 1977), p. 206.

48. Harold D. Lasswell, "Constraints on the Use of Knowledge in Decision Making," in *Information for Action,* ed. Manfred Kochen (New York: Academic Press, 1975), p. 165.

49. Charles A. O'Reilly, III, *The Intentional Distortion of Information in Organizational Communication: A Laboratory and Field Investigation* (Berkeley: Institute of Industrial Relations, University of California, 1975), NTIS Document no. AD-A020330/7GI.

50. Allen and Cohen, "Information Flow in Research and Development Laboratories," 12-19.

51. Dudley H. Dewhirst, "Influence of Perceived Information Sharing Norms on Communication Channel Utilization," *Academy of Management Journal,* 14 (September 1971): 305-15.

52. Avner M. Porat and John A. Haas, "Information Effects on Decision Making," *Behavioral Science,* 14 (March 1969): 98.

53. Kenneth Boulding, "The Ethics of Rational Decision," *Management Science,* 12 (February 1966): B161-B169.

54. Milton Roeach, *The Open and Closed Mind* (New York: Basic Books, 1960), pp. 392-93.

55. Alex Inkeles, "Problems in the Utilization of Data for Policy Making," in *Information for Action,* ed. Manfred Kochen (New York: Academic Press, 1975, p. 173.

56. Janis and Mann, *Decision Making,* p. 205.

57. George A. Miller, "The Magical Number Seven, Plus or Minus Two: Some Limits on Our Capacity for Processing Information," *Psychological Review,* 63 (March 1956): 81-97.

58. Alfred G. Smith, *Communication and Status: The Dynamics of a Research Center* (Eugene: University of Oregon, Center for the Advanced Study of Educational Administration, 1966), p. 38.

59. C. West Churchman, "Managerial Acceptance of Scientific Recommendations," in *Information for Decision Making,* ed. Alfred Rappaport (Englewood Cliffs, N.J.: Prentice Hall, 1970), p. 442.

60. John von Neumann and O. Mergenstern, *Theory of Games and Economic Behavior,* 3rd ed. (Princeton, N.J.: Princeton University Press, 1944).

61. Abraham Wald, *Statistical Decision Functions* (Bronx: Chelsea Publishing Company, 1971).

62. Thomas S. Ferguson, *Mathematical Statistics: A Decision Theoretic Approach* (New York: Academic Press, 1967), p. 5.

63. B. W. Lindgren, *Elements of Decision Theory* (New York: Macmillan Company, 1971), p. 4.

64. Colin Eden and John Harris, *Management Decision and Decison Analysis* (New York: John Wiley & Sons, 1975), pp. 63-70.

65. Terry Connolly, "Information Processing and Decision Making in Organizations," in *New Directions in Organizational Behavior,* ed. Barry M. Staw and Gerald R. Salancik (Chicago: St. Clair Press, 1977), p. 229.

66. Russell L. Ackoff, "Management Misinformation Systems," *Management Science,* 14 (December 1967): B133.

67. Walter M. Carlson, "Where Is the Payoff?" *Bulletin of the American Society for Information Science,* 4 (October 1977): 4.

68. Raymond E. Miles, *Theories of Management: Implications for Organizational Behavior and Development* (New York: McGraw-Hill, 1975), pp. 100-6; Everett M. Rogers and Rekha Agarwala-Rogers, *Communication in Organizations* (New York: The Free Press, 1976), pp. 27-58.

69. Richard K. Allen, *Organizational Management Through Communication* (New York: Harper & Row, 1977), p. 63.

70. Woody W. Horton, Jr., "Information Resources Management, Fad or Fact?" *Journal of Systems Management,* 28 (December 1977): 6-9.

71. Ackoff, "Management Misinformation Systems," B133-36.

72. Ronald J. Ebert and Terence R. Mitchell, *Organizational Decision Processes: Concepts and Analysis* (New York: Crane Russak & Company, 1975), p. 97.

73. Rensis Likert and Jane Gibson Likert, *New Ways of Managing Conflict* (New York: McGraw-Hill, 1976).

74. Ibid., pp. 128 and 121.

75. Ibid., pp. 71-106.

76. Maurice P. Marchant, *Participative Management in Academic Libraries* (Westport, Conn.: Greenwood Press, 1976).

77. Louis Kaplan, "The Literature of Participation: From Optimism to Realism," *College & Research Libraries,* 36 (November, 1975): 473-79.

78. Mulder and Henk, "Participation and Power Equalization," 430-48.

79. Victor H. Vroom and Phillip W. Yetton, *Leadership and Decision Making* (Pittsburgh: University of Pittsburgh Press, 1973), pp. 83 and 108.

80. Samuel B. Bacharach and Michael Aiken, "Communication in Administrative Bureaucracies," *Academy of Management Journal,* 20 (September 1977): 365-77.

81. Paul Sabatier, "The Acquisition and Utilization of Technical Information by Administrative Agencies," *Administrative Science Quarterly,* 23 (September 1978): 396-417.

82. Joel D. Goldhar, Louis K. Bragaw, and Jules J. Schwartz, "Information Flows, Management Styles, and Technological Innovation," *IEEE Transactions on Engineering Management,* EM 23 (February 1976): 60.

83. John R. Adams and Lloyd A. Swanson, "Information Processing Behavior and Estimating Accuracy in Operations Management," *Academy of Management Journal,* 19 (March 1976): 98-110.

84. Henry Mintzberg, "Review of *New Science of Management Decision,*" *Administrative Science Quarterly,* 22 (June 1977): 345.

85. Lyman W. Porter and Karlene H. Roberts, "Communication in Organizations," in *Handbook of Industrial and Organizational Psychology,* ed. Marvin D. Dunnette (Chicago: Rand McNally, 1976), pp. 1562-63.

86. Gerald Miller, "The Current Status of Theory and Research in Interpersonal Communication," *Human Communication,* 4 (Winter 1978): 164-78.

3
RESEARCH METHODOLOGY

INTRODUCTION

The findings presented in this volume are based on two similar research projects conducted by this writer. The first study, done in 1977, was entitled "Academic Librarians' Contact with Information Sources and Library Decision Making," henceforth referred to as the Information Contact Study. This study was conducted in four academic libraries located in the northeastern part of the United States. The second study was entitled "Academic Librarians' Evaluation of Information Sources for Library Decision Making," hereafter referred to as the Information Evaluation Study. This study was conducted in four academic libraries located in the southwestern United States. Both studies produced results related to organizational information and library decision making.

In order to better understand the findings that resulted from these studies, a discussion of the research methods employed with each may be useful. For each of these two studies a brief explanation will be made of the hypothesis and study questions that guided the research, the nature of the study environment and population, the sampling procedure, the specific data collection instruments used with each project, the data collection methods, and the techniques of data analysis that were employed, and because of the similarity of the two studies, they will be considered together. A brief discussion of the reliability and validity of the data collected will conclude the chapter.

HYPOTHESES AND RESEARCH QUESTIONS

The formulation of hypotheses serves as a guide to help determine the data to be collected and to suggest possible techniques for that collection process. Furthermore, the hypotheses provide a means to address a specific area of interest and thus limit the study to a manageable size. The primary hypothesis of the information contact study was: those people who are identified as the organizational information rich in an academic library will tend to be involved in library decision making.

In addition to obtaining data to address the above hypothesis, the study also was intended to address the following related research questions:

1. What are the social characteristics (age, sex, education, experience) and the contact with factual sources of information within the categories of administrators, public service librarians, and technical service librarians?
2. Can the factual information sources which the librarians contact be grouped into general categories or types of information?
3. What are the sociometric patterns of information seeking of the professional librarians within the academic library?

In the information evaluation study formal hypotheses as such were not addressed. However, a number of research questions were posited:

1. Will a relatively few types of information sources be constantly selected as "valuable" regardless of the specific decision situation for which they were selected?
2. Is the perceived value of specific information sources related to the librarian's administrative jobtype?
3. Are interpersonal sources of information perceived as more valuable as input for decision making than written sources?
4. Are specific information sources preferred as input for specific decision situations?
5. Can academic library decisions be categorized according to origin of the information sources (internal or external to the organization) and channel (interpersonal or written)?

The data collection instruments were developed specifically to obtain data to address the above hypothesis and research questions.

THE STUDY ENVIRONMENTS

To select academic libraries where the variables related to organizational information and decision making could be studied and to insure similarity among the libraries, the following criteria were used to determine participation in the investigation:

1. The academic library must be located at an institution of higher education where both bachelor and master's degrees are awarded.
2. The academic library must have a minimum of ten full-time professional librarians, defined as library staff members, doing work that requires special training or skills usually requiring the MLS degree or a subject master's degree.
3. The library must have a recent history of stable administrative leadership, defined as a library in which the current director has held that position for a minimum of three years.

In the information contact study a fourth criterion was added: the library must be geographically centralized, having no more than one branch library physically separated from the main library building. This criterion was added to control for organizational structure regarding sociometric patterns of information seeking.

No attempt was made to select randomly the actual libraries for study. The above criteria were employed especially to insure the study of a moderate to large, stable university library organization with a sizable number of professional librarians who are geographically centralized in a main library building. Such a study environment would be small enough for the researcher to interview the subjects himself, yet large enough to differentiate adequately among the types of information sources used by librarians as well as provide a large enough sample size to allow the use of certain statistical techniques.

Because the professional librarian and various groups of librarians are the primary level of analysis, it is essential to define the membership in such groups. The director of the library acted as final arbiter to decide if a librarian was "professional" and, thus, would participate in the study. The types of professional librarians that were included in the information contact study fall into three groups:

1. *Administrators.* The term "administrator" includes both the director of the library and, if applicable, an associate or assistant director who is charged with the responsibility of operating the library in the absence of the director. The director identified which librarian(s), if any, met this definition.
2. *Public Service Librarians.* These librarians include those professional librarians within such areas as reference and circulation, or those who spend the majority of their working time in direct contact with the patron.
3. *Technical Service Librarians.* This category includes those professional librarians within such areas as cataloging and acquisitions, or those who spend the majority of their working time not in direct contact with the patron.

In cases when there was some doubt about which group a librarian belonged in, the librarian was specifically asked if he or she spent a majority of working time in direct contact with patrons.

For the information evaluation study, the professional's administrative responsibility was categorized into four groups:

1. *Top Administration.* This term included the director and any assistant or associate directors.
2. *Department Head.* A librarian who supervises at least one other professional.
3. *Area or Section Head.* A librarian who supervises paraprofessionals but no other professionals.
4. *Nonadministration.* A librarian who does not supervise other library employees.

Based on these criteria, the librarians self-selected their appropriate category.

SAMPLING PROCEDURE

To compute the sample size needed for the two investigations, a number of factors had to be considered. First, the primary objective of the research was to do exploratory research on organizational information processing and library decision making. Second, the investigations emphasized the identification, description, and relationship between specific information-related variables as a means to better understand organizational information richness, involvement in decision making, and perceived value of information sources. Third, because of this emphasis on these variables, the selection of libraries where the variables can be studied is more important than the number of libraries and subjects selected.

With these factors in mind, the researcher utilized purposive-theoretical sampling. This type of sampling involves the use of judgment on the part of the researcher to select cases he or she thinks will best illustrate the variables under investigation. "The process does not verify the magnitude of the categories or the relationships in the population, but merely acknowledges the presence and existence of such phenomena."[1] The results from such a sampling technique are primarily intended to provide basic information about the topic so that new propositions and research questions can be formulated.

Based on the above listed factors and the criteria used to determine participation in the studies (see above), the researcher decided that each investigation would be conducted at four academic libraries (including the pre-test) with a minimum of fifty professional librarians. Such a sample size would be large enough to accomplish the primary objectives of the investigation, to address the hypothesis and research questions, and to perform certain statistical analyses. A description of the population within the academic libraries investigated for each study is presented in Table 3-1: Information Contact Study, Population; and Table 3-2: Information Evaluation Study, Population.

As previously discussed in the study environment section of this chapter, specific criteria were developed to insure the selection of academic libraries where organizational information and library decision making could be studied effectively. A total of four academic libraries were to be selected for each study: one of the four served as a site for the pre-test and in three additional libraries the study was then administered. The selection of the pre-test site followed the same procedure as for the other libraries and was based upon the same criteria.

By utilizing the most recent volumes of *Library Statistics of College and Universities*[2] and *American Library Directory*,[3] the researcher identi-

fied a pool of possible academic libraries within commuting distance that
met the criteria of having at least ten full-time professional librarians and
being located at institutions of higher education where both bachelor and
master's degrees were granted. To obtain information related to the other
criteria (administrative stability of the library, geographical centralization,
and receptiveness of the librarians to provide feedback and criticism on a
pre-test), the researcher made unobtrusive phone calls to local librarians.

TABLE 3-1

Information Contact Study, Population

LIBRARY	ADMINISTRATORS	PUBLIC SERVICE LIBRARIANS	TECHNICAL SERVICE LIBRARIANS	TOTAL
A	3	6	6	15
B	1	6	4	11
C	2	4	10	16
D	2	8	4	14
Total	8	24	24	56

TABLE 3-2

Information Evaluation Study, Population

LIBRARY	TOP ADMINISTRATORS	DEPARTMENT HEADS	SECTION HEADS	AREA HEADS	TOTAL
E	4	5	6	3	18
F	3	5	8	4	20
G	3	2	7	2	14
H	2	3	5	4	15
Total	12	15	26	13	67

INSTRUMENT: INFORMATION CONTACT STUDY

Based on the research design utilized in the Allen[4] and the Tagliacozzo[5] studies as well as the type of data needed to answer the hypothesis and related research questions of this investigation, a structured interview was developed to obtain the data (see Appendix I). This instrument was intended to obtain descriptive data about three types of variables: (1) the subject's social characteristics, (2) the subject's contact with sources of factual information, and (3) the subject's involvement in library decision making.

Previous research indicated a hesitancy on the part of some subjects to discuss where they receive information in the performance of their job. This kind of instrument would allow for each subject to be interviewed individually and for the interviewer to establish rapport with each subject, which might tend to increase the likelihood of obtaining accurate data from them.

Part II of the interview is composed of questions intended to identify the number and types of sources of information with which the subject might come into contact. These questions suggest a pool of sources of information from which the respondent can better identify his or her specific sources of information. The sources of information are categorized under the headings of professional activity, institutional activity, communication activity, and research activity. Table 3-3 summarizes the sources of information studied in Part II of the information contact study.

The pool of sources of information contains both direct sources, such as interpersonal contacts, articles read, or journals scanned, or indirect sources of information, such as professional meetings attended, memos or articles written. The indirect sources are actually *indicators* of participation in a situation where it is assumed that the person comes into contact with additional sources of information. For instance, if a person attends a professional meeting, it is assumed that he or she comes into contact with sources of information that would not have been encountered otherwise. The list of sources of information contained in Table 3-3 is based on sources identified by other researchers as well as the researcher's personal experience in an academic library. Also included in Part II of the interview is one question (number 17) intended to provide data to describe the information-seeking networks in the organization.

Part III of the interview provides data to determine if the subject is seen by the library administrator(s) as involved or not involved in library decision making. Two forms of Part III were used, one for the library administrator and a second for other professional librarians. Both forms contain a list of ten typical decision situations which many academic librarians have had to face in recent years.

TABLE 3-3

Information Contact Study: Information Sources Studied

CATEGORY	NAME OF INFORMATION SOURCE
Professional Activity	1. Professional organizational membership 2. Professional organizational committee membership 3. Professional meetings attended 4. Papers presented or talks given
Institutional Activity	5. Elected official 6. Institutional committee memberships 7. Library committee memberships
Communication Activity	8. Memos written (to employees within the library) 9. Letters/telephone calls made (outside the library) 10. Librarian interpersonal contacts 11. Paraprofessional interpersonal contacts 12. Faculty interpersonal contacts 13. Other interpersonal contacts
Research Activity	14. Size of personal collection 15. Journal subscriptions 16. Journals scanned 17. Articles read 18. Articles published 19. Books published 20. Book reviews published 21. Participation in internal library reports 22. Preparation of material for publication

The topics within this list of decision situations are purposely broad. Part III is not concerned with which topics were major decision situations for a given library but rather with providing a vehicle by which the administrators and librarians can identify the people who contributed information to help reach a decision related to a specific decision situation. Topics not specifically included in the list but which have pertinence to a given library can also be identified by the respondent and included as item numbers 11, 12, and so forth.

Administrators and librarians identified those situations about which major decisions (involving more than one department in the library) were made in the past two years or were in the process of being decided at the time of the interview. On one form, administrators identify the person on whom they most frequently relied for information for each decision situation pertaining to their library and on another form librarians indicate if they actually provided informational input to an administrator for any of the decision situations that had previously been identified as pertaining to the library. If an administrator *and* an individual librarian agree that the person provided informational input to the administrator for a specific decision situation, the person will be said to have been involved in library decision making.

INSTRUMENT: INFORMATION EVALUATION STUDY

The development of the instrument that asks respondents to evaluate information sources as input for decision making is based, in part, on the success of the information contact instrument. Because that instrument collected data on the quantity of information contacted, it was believed that the second study should concentrate on perceived quality of information sources in relation to certain typical decision situations.

The instrument was developed to be used in a survey fashion and was specifically intended to obtain data on (1) the respondents' social/administrative characteristics, (2) the subjects' perceived evaluation of various information sources as first, second, and last choice as input for typical library decisions, and (3) perceived effect of their informational input on library decision making. A copy of the instrument is presented in Appendix II.

Part II of the instrument lists twelve possible decision situations related to an academic library environment. Respondents were asked to provide their first, second, and last choice of information source to contact as an aid to analyze a specific decision situation. A list of information sources was provided from which the respondent could select the appropriate source.

The information sources investigated in the information evaluation study are similar but not identical to those examined in the information contact study. Table 3-4 presents the information sources from which the respondent could select; they are categorized according to (1) interpersonal contact, (2) written documents, (3) group or organizational sources, or (4) personal sources. Respondents could include additional sources if none of those suggested was appropriate.

The pool of information sources is intended to provide a broad range of possible choices to analyze the twelve decision situations. As with the first study, the decision situations were selected to be realistic representations of typical decisions being made in academic libraries. As such, they are used as vehicles by which the respondent's information source preferences will be meaningful. Furthermore, the instrument forces the respondent to decide which of the information sources are more or less valuable as input for specific decision situations.

DATA COLLECTION

To determine which libraries out of the pool would participate in the two investigations, initial contact was made with the directors of these libraries either by letter or telephone. In either instance, a brief explanation of the research was given to the director at that time. In some instances the director immediately agreed to have the library participate in the study: in others he or she wished first to consult with the librarians; and in still others the director immediately declined to participate. Ultimately, four academic libraries meeting the previously described criteria agreed to participate in the study.

In both investigations the first library to participate in the study served also as the site for the pre-test. In both instances the purpose of the pre-test was to determine if the data resulting from the instruments would allow the researcher to address the hypothesis and research questions and to identify any problems of ambiguity or coding with the instrument for-

mat. In general, their criticism indicated that the questions were clearly
understood, but they did suggest some minor wording changes in some
questions. They noted that their responses in many cases were only
estimated, but believed that the estimates were accurate representations
of contacts with and perceived value of various information sources.

TABLE 3-4

Information Evaluation Study: Information Sources Studied

CATEGORY	NAME OF INFORMATION SOURCE
Interpersonal Contact (with)	1. Professional staff in library
	2. Paraprofessional staff in library
	3. Library patrons (users)
	4. Librarians *outside* the library
	5. Faculty members
	6. Vendors, jobbers, salespersons
Written Documents	7. Books
	8. Articles from library-related periodicals or journals
	9. Book reviews
	10. Articles from journals not related directly to librarianship
	11. Brochures, advertisements, flyers, etc.
	12. Reports or statistical information produced by staff members in your library
Group or Organizational	13. Committee or group meetings composed of library staff members
	14. Committee or group meetings with nonlibrary staff members
	15. Committee or group meetings of professional organizations (ALA, etc.)
Personal	16. Continuing education
	17. Past experiences
	18. Personal opinion
	19. Do some research on my own to analyze decision situation
	20. Other: _____

At the participating libraries a memo was circulated to the professional librarians announcing the dates of the researcher's visit to the library, describing the general nature of the research, and asking them for their cooperation. For each library in both investigations a date was agreed upon when the researcher would come to the library and administer the instrument.

For the information contact study a schedule was developed assigning appointments for each librarian with the researcher. The average time for each interview was forty-five minutes, and two to three days were required to interview all librarians at a given library. The interview began after the respondent had been assured that all responses would be confidential and under no circumstances would (1) the name of the library be divulged, (2) the names of individual librarians be divulged, or (3) the information provided by a respondent be given to other members of the library.

Each subject was asked to complete Part I of the interview alone by filling in the blanks on the questionnaire. Then the researcher asked each question from the interview and wrote the responses of the subject on the questionnaire. To increase the reliability of the respondent's answers to Part II of the questionnaire, each respondent was asked to provide specific enumerations to each question.

The completion of Part III of the interview was accomplished by showing the respondent the list of typical decision situations and asking him or her to put an "X" next to those decision situations that pertained to that library during the past two years. For each major decision situation that pertained to the library, the librarian next indicated if he or she had provided information about that decision situation to an administrator either in the form of a written document or through interpersonal communication. Administrators, on the other hand, listed the name of the person on whom they had most frequently relied for information pertaining to any decision situations he or she had previously identified as relating to the library in the past two years.

Specific attention was given to defining a major decision situation as one involving two or more departments in the library and explaining that it was not necessary for an actual decision to have been reached for identificaton of a major decision situation. Additionally, the researcher indicated that it did not matter whether the decision was made in favor or against the position of the respondent; the question was, Did you provide informational input to a library administrator for a specific decision situation?

After completion of the interview, the librarian would notify the next person on the schedule that the room was now vacant. In this manner all the librarians were interviewed. Each respondent was assured that names would not be revealed but had to be obtained in order to do sociometric analysis and that responses made by an individual would not be divulged to any other member in the organization. The response rate for usable returns for the four participating libraries in the information contact study was 56 of 57 librarians, or 98 percent.

The data collection process for the second study, information evaluation, was less complex than that for the first study. After agreeing upon a date for the researcher to visit the library, all the librarians gathered together in one room and met with the researcher. At that time the researcher explained the nature of the research to the participants, assured them of the confidentiality of their responses, and distributed a questionnaire to each to be completed during the session.

Typically, a session at each library lasted forty-five minutes to one hour. The researcher remained in the room and answered any questions regarding the completion of the questionnaire. When an individual had completed the questionnaire it was given to the researcher.

Not all the librarians in all instances could attend the scheduled meeting because of prior commitments or the need to maintain service points throughout the library. In such cases a copy of the questionnaire with a self-addressed stamped envelope was given to an administrator to be distributed to the absent librarians. After a one-week period a follow-up reminder was sent to the librarians asking them to complete the questionnaire if they had not as yet done so.

As a result of both the on-site data collection and those returned by mail, sixty-six completed questionnaires were obtained, out of a total population of seventy-five professional librarians from these four libraries. Thus, the response rate of usable returns was 89 percent.

ANALYSIS OF DATA

To expedite the data analysis process, the data were processed for the most part by using *SPSS: Statistical Package for the Social Sciences.*[6] Various forms of descriptive statistics, use of factor analysis, and tests of significance were employed to examine the relationships between variables and address the hypothesis and research questions.

Data collected in the information contact study were used to describe two key variables, organizational information richness and involvement in decision making. Based on their number of contacts with information sources, each subject was ascribed an additive score. The score is an indicator of the person's contact with sources of information compared to other individuals in the organization.

This analysis provides an index composed of subjects within the library ranked in order of their total number of contacts with sources of information. The organizational information rich were defined as those people who rank in the top 50 percent of the scores for each individual library. Those people who ranked in the bottom 49 percent were defined as the organizational information poor. For example, if an academic library has ten professional librarians whose contacts with factual information sources are 96, 85, 77, 72, 51, 48, 35, 31, 26, and 14, the top five librarians (or top 50 percent) will be identified as organizational information rich.

Involvement in decision making is determined by examining the administrators' and librarians' responses to Part III of the interview. All administrators are assumed a priori to be involved in decision making because of their position in the organization. During the interview the researcher specifically defined who were administrators for that library. If the administrator and the librarian agreed that the librarian provided informational input for a specific decision situation to an administrator in the library, the person was identified as involved in decision making.

As a result of these two procedures, each person in a library was classified as (1) information rich or information poor, and (2) involved in library decision making or not involved in library decision making. A contingency table was drawn to summarize the data in terms of these classifications. A standard statistical test can determine the degree to which the results fit an expected multinominal distribution and indicate the probability that such a distribution would occur.

The data from the information contact study also can be used to determine if categories of information can be identified through factor analysis. Factor analysis addresses itself to the study of interrelationships among a total set of observed variables. In a sense, each of the observed variables in factor analysis is considered as a dependent variable that is a function of some underlying, latent, and hypothetical set of factors. The use of factor analysis to examine the variables that compose the potential sources of information will suggest possible underlying or unifying relationships (categories) among the sources of information, if they exist.

The information-seeking networks of the four libraries that participated in the information contact study were depicted with sociometric mapping. Individuals were coded as being opinion leaders, participants, or isolates in each network. Once these groups are identified, their characteristics can be compared to other groups, such as administrators, public service librarians, technical service librarians, information rich, and information poor.

The survey instrument used in the information evaluation study was intended to survey the selection of various information sources and not to create measures for certain variables as in the information contact study. Therefore, specific analysis techniques were not needed for the description of operational variables. Standard descriptive statistics were used to analyze the respondent's choice of information sources. Relationships between types of information sources and specific decision situations were tested by chi-square analysis. Selection of information sources was analyzed by categorizing them as internal/external or interpersonal/written. Because the data were categorical or nominal, sophisticated tests and procedures such as factor analysis were not appropriate.

In short, the survey data from the information evaluation study were exploratory and formal hypothesis testing was not done, although the analysis of data does address the research questions. The analysis of data, therefore, is largely descriptive and is intended to describe existing information source preferences and to provide a basis for the future generation of hypotheses related to the perceived value of information sources, administrative jobtypes and selection of sources, and categories of decision situations based on information source selection.

A NOTE ON THE RELIABILITY
AND VALIDITY OF THE DATA

Reliability implies stability and consistency of measurement—accuracy. Three criteria can be suggested for reliable measurement. The first criterion is the selection of specific questions that represent all possible questions regarding the phenomenon being measured. The fact that the researcher

has selected a specific sample of questions introduces a degree of inconsistency. If the sample contained all possible questions in the universe, the
inconsistency would disappear. Therefore, the more representative the
questions in the sample are, the higher the questionnaire's reliability will
be.[7]

On this criterion, the questions related to information sources should
be quite reliable since they were intended to sample all possible sources
of information. In both the information contact study and the information evaluation study, the pre-test determined that additional types of
information sources contacted or evaluated by libraries could not be
identified.

A second criterion to determine reliable measurement is the accurate
scoring or coding of responses by the researcher. Three actions were taken
to increase the consistency of scoring. First, respondents were encouraged
to ask for clarification of any terms or questions that seemed unclear;
second, all interviews and survey administration was done by one person;
and third, a written set of definitions/descriptions of information sources
was maintained throughout the data collection process in both studies.

A third criterion that may be used as an indicator of reliability is to
compute a coefficient of reliability. There are a number of reliability coefficients that have been suggested, but each coefficient, in general, ex-
presses the ratio of the true score variance (perfect reliability with no
error) to the observed score variance.[8] The coefficient of reliability that
was used for the information contact study is one developed by Kuder
and Richardson and may be calculated with a knowledge of the mean
and variance of the scores plus the number of items on the test.

The Kuder-Richardson formula was applied to Part II of the information contact study instrument. The coefficients of reliability, computed
on an individual library basis, ranged from .41 to .53. Although there is no
rule of thumb that will tell when the coefficient is "high enough," Jum
C. Nunally suggests that instruments with a reliability coefficient of .50
to .60 have moderate reliability and often suffice for purposes of measurement.[9]

Because the data from the information evaluation study is generally of
a categorical level, the computation of a reliability coefficient is not appropriate. However, an indicator of the reliability of the responses for the
selection of information sources can be suggested. A contingency table of
19 X 12 (types of information sources by number of decision situations)

can be used to summarize respondents' first-choice selection of an information source for a given decision situation.

One can assume that if the data were unreliable, random responses throughout the contingency table would be evident. Thus, the null hypothesis is that the selections of information sources are random responses and, therefore, unreliable. However, a chi-square goodness-of-fit test rejects this hypothesis at the .01 level of significance. Thus, the responses are not random. Indeed, this procedure does not in itself establish reliability, it merely verifies the conditions necessary for the data to be reliable.

Based on the criteria of complete and representative questions, accurate and consistent scoring, coefficient of reliability, and the rejection of the hypothesis that the data are random responses, both instruments appear to have a moderate degree of reliability. Evaluation of reliability based on these criteria *indicate* adequate reliability for purposes of exploratory research related to organizational information and academic library decision making.

The validity of the instrument is the extent to which it accurately measures what it purports to measure.[10] A measure may be reliable and still be invalid. Validity cannot be established beyond a shadow of a doubt; criteria are established and indicators suggesting the relative degree of validity demonstrated.

One criterion of internal validity is that of face validity. Face validity is a conceptual criterion which simply asks for (1) a representative collection of test items, and (2) "sensible" methods of test construction and administration. If users of the test and people knowledgeable about the topic agree that the method and the instrument were sound and well administered—as they did in the case of these two studies—the measures are said to have face validity.[11]

Convergent validity is likely when certain measures show similar distribution of variables among respondents.[12] Factor analysis is an excellent tool to compare such distributions. For the information contact study, five samples of the same data were examined. In each sample factor 1 and factor 2 consistently identified the same variables as responsible for variance explained.

Because of the nature of the data (categorical) from the information evaluation study, factor analysis or other meaningful indicators of similar distributions of variables could not be performed. Therefore, no indicator of convergent validity has been provided.

A final criterion of validity is the degree to which the results can be generalized to the population as a whole. Generalizability is largely dependent on the sampling procedure, the selection of study sites, and the characteristics of the participants in the study.

In short, academic libraries that meet the criteria of (1) being at an institution awarding at least bachelors and masters degrees, (2) having a minimum of ten full-time professional librarians, (3) having stable administrative leadership, and (4) being geographically centralized will find the results of these two studies to be more valid for their particular situation than those libraries not meeting the criteria.

Furthermore, it is the belief of this writer that the libraries participating in this study represent the typical medium-large sized academic library in the United States in terms of organizational structure, budget, collection sizes, and nature of the individual librarians. Therefore, the results from these studies should be generalizable to a number of academic librarians and libraries in the United States.

SUMMARY

A carefully constructed research methodology was employed to collect data in two similar studies related to organizational information and library decision making: (1) the information contact study, and (2) the information evaluation study. Both studies were conducted at medium-large sized academic libraries, one in the northeastern part of the United States, and the second in the Southwest.

Hypotheses and research questions guided the development of data collection instruments. The information contact study utilized an interview format; the information evaluation study utilized a survey questionnaire. Purposeful theoretical sampling was employed to identify librarians to participate in the studies. Various descriptive statistics and tests of significance of relationships between variables through SPSS were used to analyze the data. Based on specific criteria of reliability and validity, the results appear to be consistent, accurate, and, within limitations, generalizable.

NOTES

1. Nan Lin, *Foundations of Social Research* (New York: McGraw-Hill, 1976), pp. 158-59.

2. *Library Statistics of Colleges and Universities: Fall 1973,* 2 vols. (Washington, D.C.: National Center for Education Statistics, 1976).

3. *American Library Directory, 1976-1977* (New York: Bowker, 1976).

4. T. J. Allen and S. I. Cohen, "Information Flow in Research and Development Laboratories," *Administrative Science Quarterly,* 14 (March 1969): 12-19.

5. Renita Tagliacozzo, Manfred Kochen, and William Everett, "The Use of Information by Decision Makers in Public Service Organizations," in *Communication for Decision Makers, Proceedings of the American Society for Information Science,* vol. 8, ed. Jeanne B. North (Westport, Conn.: Greenwood Press, 1971), pp. 55-57.

6. *SPSS: Statistical Package for the Social Sciences,* 2nd ed. (New York: McGraw-Hill, 1975).

7. D. K. Witka, ed., *Handbook of Measurement and Assessment in Behavior Sciences,* 2nd ed. (Reading, Mass.: Addison-Wesley, 1968), pp. 267-68.

8. John T. Roscoe, *Fundamental Research Statistics for Behavioral Sciences,* 2nd ed. (New York: Holt Rinehart and Winston, 1975), p. 132.

9. Jum C. Nunally, *Psychometric Theory* (New York: McGraw-Hill, 1967), p. 80.

10. William J. Paisley, *Behavioral Studies of Scientific Information Flow: An Appendix on Method* (Stanford, Calif.: Stanford University, 1969), pp. A-2 through A-6 (mimeograph).

11. Nunally, *Psychometric Theory,* p. 80.

12. Nan Lin, *Foundations of Social Research, pp. 174-5.*

4
CONTACT WITH
INFORMATION SOURCES

INTRODUCTION

In order to better understand the relationship between information
sources and the decision-making process, a closer examination of an individual's "information potential" is necessary. Information potential is
composed of two parts, the first being the ability of the individual to put
him- or herself in such a position as to contact various information sources
that are likely to be related to the operations and services provided by the
organization. The second aspect of an individual's information potential
is the ability to select appropriate information sources to resolve a specific
decision situation affecting the organization.

Thus, it may be suggested that every organizational member has two
related, but different, components that affect his or her ability to provide
informational input into the decision-making process. Contact with information sources may be seen as a reservoir of sources the person maintains for no particular reason other than, perhaps, an intuitive feeling that
since such sources have been useful in the past, they will be useful in the
performance of the job at some point in the future.

This stockpiling of information is evident in the personal files of the
employee, the subscription to certain professional journals, and the desire
to be a part of certain committees or other interpersonal communication.
In short, this first component of information potential is the information environment in which the person becomes immersed. It is this founda-

tion that largely determines whether a person, when confronted with a specific decision situation affecting the organization, will seek and select additional information related to that topic.

Assuming that this concept of information potential is a useful framework of analysis, an organizational member may provide informational input to a given decision situation based *only* on previous contacts with information, or he or she may decide to select additional sources which, in the opinion of the individual, will specifically address a particular decision situation. Thus, the second component contributing to information potential is the person's ability to select additional information sources to resolve a specific decision situation.

Within this second component of information potential, questions of value or, more correctly, perceived value of specific types of information sources are raised. Based on the nature of the decision situation and previous information contacts, the individual may select information sources perceived to be "valuable," that is, likely to reduce or resolve the uncertainty surrounding a specific decision situation. Ultimately, the value of the source is determined by its ability to increase the effectiveness or efficiency of various organizational operations as a result of improved informational input into the decision-making process. This topic of selecting information sources is the second component of information potential and will be addressed in Chapter 6.

The distinction between an information source being contacted for stockpiling and an information source being selected as input for a specific decision situation may be somewhat unclear. The primary distinction between the two is that of initial motive. Was the information source acquired first because it was to be used for a specific identifiable decision situation? If so, it may be considered as a selected source rather than a contacted source, even though it may ultimately serve as both.

This concept of information potential appears to be appropriate when examining a clearly identifiable profession or occupation such as librarianship. It may be suggested that individuals who work in a similar organizational environment as part of the same larger profession contact information sources and select additional sources from a relatively stable range of sources. One might expect considerable overlap of information sources that are contacted and those that are selected. Such is the finding in this study. However, once these sources are identified it may be possible to address this concept of information potential.

This chapter will examine contacts with information sources by a group of academic librarians. The data presented come from the information contact study previously described. The number and types of contacts for various types of librarians will be presented, as well as a discussion of the range of information sources typically contacted by academic librarians. Categories of information sources will be suggested based on these contacts. The chapter will conclude by suggesting that the academic librarians' contact with information sources may be described best as that of a generalist.

INFORMATION SOURCES CONTACTED

To determine an estimate of an academic librarian's contact with information sources, or an estimate of his or her reservoir of information, a list of twenty-two typical sources/situations was developed. Librarians were then interviewed and asked to identify which sources they had contacted within a certain recent time period. This technique identified both specific information sources and certain situations in which it can be assumed that the individual contacted information because of that situation—such as preparing a work for publication.

The sources/situations examined are listed in Table 3-3 and were categorized into four areas of activity. The first is professional activity, which includes participation in various professional organizations related to librarianship or to the nature of the individual's position. To be considered as a member, the librarian had to pay dues or be listed on some official roster. Attendance at a professional meeting would include any activity related, in a broad sense, to librarianship but must include at least state or regional representation. Papers presented included speeches, panel discussions, or other planned presentations at a professional meeting.

The second category of information contacts relates to institutional activity. A person was considered to be an elected official if either elected or appointed to an official position in a professional organization, in the library, or in the college or university. Institutional committee membership included activity in any formally constituted group that had primarily university membership. Library committee membership was limited to only group activity on committees or advisory boards within the library.

The third category is communication activity and includes the number of memos written to other employees in the library and the number of letters or telephone calls made to individuals outside the library. Communication activity also includes interpersonal contacts, that is, face to face or telephone contact with (1) other professionals in the library, (2) paraprofessionals in the library, (3) teaching faculty or college/university administrators, or (4) other individuals such as vendors or community officials. For an interpersonal contact to be counted as part of the respondent's total score, the conversation had to be related to the respondent's job performance, organization, or profession.

The final area of information contact has to do with research activity. Within this category an attempt was made to determine the size of the individual's personal collection of material related to librarianship or his or her specific area of responsibility. Collection size was weighted as follows: 1 equals a collection size of 0 to 10 items; 2 equals 11 to 25 items; 3 equals 26 to 50 items; 4 equals 51 to 100 items; 5 equals 101 to 250 items; and 6 equals 251 or more items. An item was considered to be a book, journal, report, or other piece of written material. In short, those individuals with a larger personal collection were given a higher score in terms of estimating information contact.

The category of research activity also included the number of professional journals to which the individual personally subscribed, the number of journals that the individual regularly scanned, and the number of articles within each of these that the individual actually read. Research activity also included the number of books, articles, and book reviews the individual had published during the past two years. In addition, this category determined if the individual was involved in the writing of any in-house studies, reports, or proposals related to the operation of the library or the number of items an individual was currently preparing for publication. At the minimum, at least an outline had to be evidenced to count toward preparation of an item for publication.

An indicator of a person's information contact was determined by adding up the number of all information sources with which he or she came into contact. Despite various formats, channels, media, and time span, each factor or situation was considered as a potential contact with information, and the total number of sources/situations was computed for each subject. To compare the information contact of the individuals, an index was prepared which would rank each subject by his or her total number of information sources.

It is important to recognize the assumptions and limitations of such an index. The unifying factor of these various information sources/situations is that they all are, *by definition,* sources of information contact. The score of each person indicates the person's information reservoir or relationship with the information environment. Because the sources/situations are similar for all librarians, the score provides a means to compare one individual's contact with that of another.

Abraham Kaplan has pointed out four requirements to allow for additive measurements: the operation must be commutative, associative, incremental, and satisfy a requirement of equality.[1] A score based on such an additive measurement hinges on the assumption that the various sources of information can have a similar *potential* impact on an individual. Such an assumption is required because of our inability, at this time, to differentiate among the cognitive filters applied to various sources when contacted by an individual. Furthermore, the score also assumes an arbitrary rating by which a person receives more "credit" each time that person comes into contact with an information source.

Based on this score it is possible to describe the information environment of academic librarians. Only information sources/situations that are related to the performance of an individual's job, organization, or profession have been considered in this score. It is recognized that such a score is only an *indicator* of the relative information contacts librarians have with a selected, albeit broad, range of possible information sources/situations. As such, however, it serves as the basis for examining the first component of an academic librarian's information potential.

CONTACT WITH SPECIFIC INFORMATION SOURCES

Academic librarians' contact with information may be better understood in light of their background characteristics. Table 4-1 describes the group characteristics of administrators, technical service librarians, and public service librarians. In this sample, it is evident that most of the administrators were male; they had more years of experience both in that particular library and in the profession than the other two groups; and they are better educated than other librarians.

TABLE 4-1

Group Characteristics of Administrators, Technical
Service Librarians, and Public Service Librarians

	ADMINISTRATORS (8)	PUBLIC SERVICE LIBRARIANS (24)	TECHNICAL SERVICE LIBRARIANS (24)
Sex (%)			
male	75	54	33
female	25	46	67
Average Age	50	40	41
Average Number of Years of Library Employment	12	7	8
Average Number of Years of Professional Experience	15	9	11
Education (%)*			
B.A.	0	8	0
M.L.S.	38	54	83
M.L.S.+**	37	37	13
Ph.D.	25	0	4
Average Number of Contacts with Factual Sources of Information	90	54	40
Average Rank in Library Based on Information Contact	3	7	10

* Figures may not always total 100% due to rounding.
** M.L.S.+ includes those librarians with two or more subject master's degrees.

The characteristics of public service librarians and technical service librarians are remarkably similar except for education. Their average age, years of library employment, and professional employment are almost the same. Differences occur in sex—a greater percentage of public service librarians are male—and education—public service librarians are better educated. Overall, it is clear that there is a substantial difference between the groups in their contact with information. Administrators contact substantially more sources than either of the other two groups, and public service librarians contact more sources than technical service librarians.

An overview of the average number of contacts with information sources by librarian jobtype is presented in Table 4-2. In this figure each of the twenty-two information sources/situations is used as a means to describe the librarian's contact. Average number of contacts for specific information sources between public service librarians and technical service librarians is, once again, quite similar except for one general category of sources: interpersonal communication.

Comparing interpersonal communication activity between the two groups, it is apparent that public service librarians initiate more letters or telephone calls outside the library, have substantially more interpersonal contact with faculty and college/university administrators, and have more interpersonal contacts with others such as vendors and community individuals. Indeed, these three categories of contact account for most of the differences in information contact between the two groups.

Closer examination of interpersonal contacts between these two groups also suggests that both have similar contact with other librarians and paraprofessionals *in the library.* However, technical service librarians' contact with external or nonlibrary interpersonal sources is substantially less than that of the other two groups. Such interpersonal communication on the part of technical service librarians suggests their dependence on internally generated information and limited interpersonal contact with other professionals or individuals knowledgeable about librarianship from outside the library.

The most striking aspect of the administrators' contact with information is that their overall average score is almost twice that of the average academic librarian. In general, they contact more sources than other librarians in a number of categories. However, the administrators write substantially more memos (internally) and write more letters and make more

TABLE 4-2

Average Number of Contacts with Information
Sources by Librarian Jobtype

	ADMINI-STRATORS (8)	PUBLIC SERVICE LIBRARIANS (24)	TECHNICAL SERVICE LIBRARIANS (24)
1. Professional organizational membership	2.8	2.0	1.1
2. Professional organizational committee membership	.8	.4	.3
3. Professional meetings attended in last year	3.3	4.5	2.4
4. Papers, speeches, etc. presented at meetings during past year	.6	.1	.1
5. Elected positions in organizations at this time	1.1	.5	.5
6. Membership in college/university committees	2.5	1.0	1.3
7. Membership in library committees	2.0	1.0	1.0
8. Memos per day to library organizational members	3.8	1.3	1.8

9. Letters or telephone calls per day made outside the library	11.6	4.5	2.5
10. Interpersonal contacts per day with library professionals	7.8	4.6	4.7
11. Interpersonal contacts per day with library paraprofessionals	3.3	4.5	1.0
12. Interpersonal contacts per day with faculty/administrators	4.8	2.9	3.2
13. Interpersonal contacts per day with others (vendors, etc.)	2.3	4.2	1.2
14. Size of personal collection (see text for explanation)	2.8	3.1	2.4
15. Journals currently subscribed to	2.1	2.0	1.4
16. Journals regularly scanned	5.2	5.2	4.0
17. Articles read per month	14.6	8.6	7.6
18. Articles published in last two years	.6	0	0
19. Book reviews published in last two years	5.8	.5	.5
20. Books published in last two years	0	0	0
21. Internal studies/reports in last two years	12.2	2.4	3.5
22. Items being prepared for publication	.6	.2	.1
AVERAGE TOTAL*	90.0	54.0	40.0

*Figures may not always equal the total due to rounding.

telephone calls (externally) than the other two groups. Furthermore, they read substantially more articles and write more book reviews, internal reports, or studies than do the other professional librarians.

The heavy reliance of administrators on "the literature" both in terms of articles read and internal reports produced is interesting in light of a recent study by T. J. Allen. In the study, Allen suggests two critical purposes of a professional literature: (1) a source of ideas, and (2) a means of problem definition.[2] Typically, these purposes are addressed during initial stages of decision making. Based on these two criteria, other librarians do not appear to be as well-prepared for the initial stages of library decision making.

Furthermore, it is also interesting to note the informal comments made during the interviews by each of these groups regarding contact with the professional literature. Both public and technical service librarians indicated skepticism and cynicism about the overall usefulness of the literature, whereas administrators frequently commented on its value. In a number of instances, individual administrators set aside specific time periods during the week to examine recent journals and other publications.

A number of factors support the administrator's contact with large amounts of factual information simply because he or she is an administrator. Administrators are likely to control travel budgets and thus attend more professional meetings than other librarians; they are likely to have a larger salary, which may allow the purchase of more information sources than other librarians can afford, and their status within the organization is likely to encourage them to be the first persons to examine the new journals, books, or other recent acquisitions. Additionally, a person who is an administrator may be expected to serve on a number of university, professional, or library committees simply because he or she holds that position in the library.

Although there is substantial discrepancy among the three groups in their overall total contact with information sources, the relative contact with types of sources compared to other sources is remarkably similar in all three groups. Table 4-3 summarizes the percent of total information contact for the three groups of librarians in terms of professional activity, institutional activity, communication activity, and research activity. A chi-square test confirms the obvious: there is no significant difference between jobtype and contact with these categories of information sources.

Stated differently, Table 4-3 suggests that all three groups of librarians come into contact with the same relative percentage of information sources within categories of professional activity, institutional activity, communication activity, and research activity. The primary difference is that administrators contact substantially more *total sources* than public service librarians, who, in turn, contact more *total sources* than technical service librarians.

Another implication of Table 4-3 is that the types of sources that make up the reservoir of information sources for administrators, public service librarians, and technical service librarians are basically the same for each. While it is possible that each group may have different purposes or information needs, they satisfy those needs from a similar reservoir of information contact. Indeed, the discrepancy among the groups in total contact may be explained, in part, by different information needs.

The range of total number of contacts with information sources for librarians studied is summarized in Figure 4-1. As the figure suggests, the range is quite broad—from a minimum of eight to a maximum of 150. Keeping in mind that these scores represent contact from the same list of sources over similar periods of time, one might be surprised at the significant differences among the librarians' total scores. Clearly, librarians in the organizations investigated do not have similar information potential, at least in their information contacts.

TABLE 4-3

Percent of Total Information Contact for Each Jobtype

Information Contact	Administrators	Public Service Librarians	Technical Service Librarians
Professional Activity (items 1-4)	8	12	9
Institutional Activity (items 5-7)	6	7	7
Communication Activity (items 8-13)	37	40	36
Research Activity (items 14-22)	49	41	48

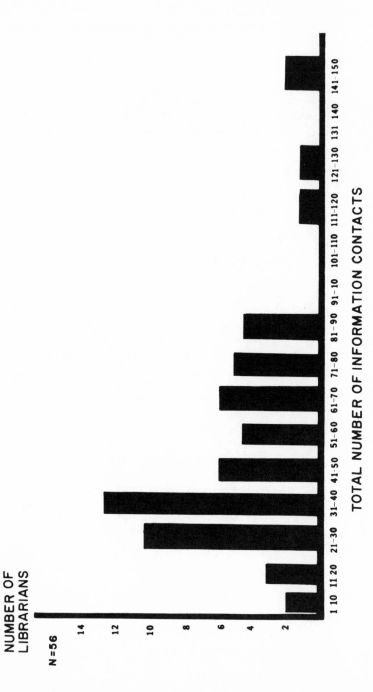

FIGURE 4-1 Range of Total Number of Contacts with Information Sources for All Librarians

To understand this broad number of sources contacted, a return to the actual interviews is instructive. When reporting few or no contacts with specific sources, the librarian usually felt obligated to justify the response. The majority of such rationalization took the position that contacting a specific source was not necessary either because (1) there was nothing "new" or "useful" from such sources for the individual, or (2) such sources were not necessary for the person to perform his or her job in the library.

Such a stance is indeed paradoxical for the professional librarian. Because the profession is one in which the importance of various types of information, of organizing information, and disseminating information is inherent in the professional philosophy, it does seem strange that they, in effect, "knock their own product." Furthermore, this position suggests that for some librarians information will not be contacted until it is "necessary." Communication researchers suggest that a broad range of contact with different types of information is a prerequisite for creativity and idea generation.[3]

Thus, the information environment of academic librarians is substantially different in terms of each one's overall contact with information sources. Although all librarians seem to contact the same basic pool of sources some librarians appear to contact substantially more sources than other librarians. And while broad categories of information sources appear to have the same relative contact with librarians, there are some differences as to specific sources that are contacted. Technical service librarians are less likely to contact external interpersonal sources and administrators are more likely to write internal reports/studies, book reviews, and memos as well as have more contact with written sources such as journal articles.

CATEGORIES OF INFORMATION
SOURCES CONTACTED

An area of interest to this investigation is the identification of general categories of sources of information with which professional librarians come into contact. Can the sources of information be grouped into broad or general types of information? A. G. Smith has suggested that for members of a university research center information sources can be categorized as either research or administrative in nature.[4]

Administrative sources are more formal communication methods such as memos, committee meetings, or other internal organizational documents. Research sources tend to be scholarly or professional. For purposes of this investigation, administrative sources are generally used for the operation of the organization as a whole whereas research sources are used to enhance the research or technical skills of the individual. Based on Smith's research, this notion has been applied to librarians. Information sources have been defined as either administrative or research. The categorization of the sources of information is based on Smith's research and the researcher's personal experience. Table 4-4 summarizes the types of information sources in each category.

If one assumes an unlimited number of possible factual sources of information for a given librarian regardless of specific location, a summary of administrative/research sources for all fifty-six respondents can be presented to compare the relationship of administrative/research sources for librarians grouped as administrators, public service librarians, and technical service librarians. Table 4-5 presents the breakdown of administrative/research sources of information for each jobtype.

This approach to identifying broad groups of information sources is deductive in that it assigns, a priori, information sources to specific groups. An inductive approach does not make any a priori assumptions but looks for empiricial indicators of information source relationships. The procedure of factor analysis is well suited to such a purpose and was used as a technique to analyze the factual sources of information for possible broad groupings.

Although factor analysis can be a powerful statistical tool, it must be used with caution, especially for relatively small sample sizes as in this investigation. The researcher must carefully select the variables to undergo factor analysis since factor analysis assumes at least ordinal level data. Additionally, a general rule of thumb informally suggested to this researcher is that there should be at least twice as many cases as variables for meaningful analysis to take place.

In order to improve the validity of the procedure in this instance, information sources (variables) that were measured on a nominal scale as well as those whose variance and mean approached zero were eliminated from the analysis; thus, a total of seventeen variables was analyzed by factor analysis.

TABLE 4-4

Information Sources Categorized as
Administrative or Research in Nature

	ADMINISTRATIVE		RESEARCH
Item	Description	Item	Description
1	Professional organization membership	14	Size of personal collection
2	Professional organization committee membership	15	Journal subscriptions
		16	Journals scanned
3	Professional meetings attended	17	Articles read
4	Papers/speeches presented	18	Articles published
5	Elected official	19	Books published
6	Institutional committee membership	20	Book reviews published
7	Library committee membership	21	Library reports/internal studies
8	Memos written (inside library)	22	Preparation of material for publication
9	Telephone calls, letters written (outside library)		
10-13	Interpersonal contacts		
	(a) with professional librarians		
	(b) with paraprofessional librarians		
	(c) with college-university faculty/ administrators		
	(d) other		

TABLE 4-5

Average Number of Contacts with Administrative/
Research Information Sources by Jobtype

	ADMINISTRATIVE SOURCES	RESEARCH SOURCES	TOTAL SOURCES
Administrators	46	43	89
Public Service Librarians	32	22	54
Technical Service Librarians	20	20	40

Because there are a number of different procedures possible under the general heading "factor analysis," it is important to note the specific technique used in this investigation. The most widely accepted factoring method is principal factoring with iteration, known as PA2 in the SPSS program. This method replaces the main diagonal elements of the correlation matrix with communality estimates based on the squared multiple correlation between a given variable and other variables being factored. This process continues until the differences between the two successive communality estimates are negligible or until any of the communalities exceeds 1.0— at which point the previous iteration is retained.[5] The factor analysis done in this investigation is based on the above technique.

The factor analysis identified two factors (or underlying variables) that, taken together, explain 65 percent of the total variance. The factor loadings, eigenvalues, and variance explained from the factor analysis of the seventeen variables (information sources) suggest a second kind of source categorization. For each factor the variables were individually analyzed. Those variables that had factor loadings of .4 or higher were deemed to be significant, that is, more important than other variables in explaining what the factor actually measured.

The identification of two factors which, taken together, explain upwards of 65 percent of the total variance is most significant. A closer examination of the specific sources each factor is actually measuring (variables with loadings of .4 or higher) indicates that the origin of the information sources in factor 2 are inside the library whereas those from factor 1 are outside the library. In short, the underlying or latent dimension of the information sources as identified by factor analysis is the origin of the information source—either internal or external to the library. Table 4-6 summarizes the variables within each factor.

Because factor analysis is a complex procedure and "a factor analysis of randomly generated data will seem to make some sense if stared at long enough and hopefully enough,"[6] this researcher applied internal checks to increase the confidence in the results. Specifically, five different factor analyses were performed on various subgroups of the cases. In all instances, the two factors continued to explain between 59 percent and 65 percent of the total variance. More important, the same variables for each factor were repeatedly found to have factor loadings of .4 or higher.

Based on the groupings of information sources as either internal or external and using the variables (information sources) in the factor analysis as criteria, a computation of average number of internal/external sources of information for librarians grouped as administrators, public service librarians, or technical service librarians can be made. Table 4-7 summarizes the average number of contacts with internal/external information sources by jobtype.

TABLE 4-6

Variables with Factor Loadings of .4 or Higher

EXTERNAL	INTERNAL
1. Professional organizational memberships	1. Memos written
2. Professional organizational committee memberships	2. Interpersonal contacts with professional librarians
3. Professional meetings attended	3. Interpersonal contacts with paraprofessionals
4. Institutional committee memberships	4. Interpersonal contacts with faculty
5. Journal subscriptions	5. Interpersonal contacts with others
6. Articles read	
7. Book reviews published	

TABLE 4-7

Average Number of Contacts with Internal/External
Information Sources by Jobtype

	INTERNAL SOURCES	EXTERNAL SOURCES	TOTAL SOURCES
Administrators	36	42	78
Public Service Librarians	22	22	44
Technical Service Librarians	16	13	29

A comparison between average administrative/research information
sources (Table 4-5) and average internal/external information sources
(Table 4-7) contacted by librarians shows a number of similarities. First,
all three groups of librarians retain a relative balance between internal/
external sources (as they did with administrative/research sources) and
second, the rank of the groups stays the same—administrators come into
contact with more sources of information than public service librarians,
who, in turn, contact more sources than technical service librarians. These
similarities become more striking when one considers that twenty-two
variables (information sources) were used to compute administrative/
research sources and only twelve variables were used to compute inter-
nal/external sources of information.

For professional librarians in this sample, information sources/situations
may be categorized as either administrative/research or internal/external.
The first categorization is suggested on a deductive basis but is not supported by empirical evidence generated by factor analysis. Regardless
of the grouping criteria used, administrators, public service librarians,
and technical service librarians scored remarkably the same in terms of
their nonpreference for specific information source categories as well as
their relative ranking among average group contacts with information
sources.

Thus, an analysis of categories of information sources contacted by
academic librarians reinforces the results from the analysis of total contacts with information sources. The categories—however one wishes to

define them—remain as a basic reservoir from which the librarian contacts the information environment and determines, in part, his or her information potential. This reservoir of information appears to be unique, more so because of its broad and general characteristics than for its specific channel or format type.

THE ACADEMIC LIBRARIAN AS GENERALIST

Regardless of jobtype, academic librarians in this investigation came into contact with a wide variety of types of information sources. No significant relationships were identified between contacts with *types* of sources or *categories* of sources and jobtypes. The primary difference among jobtypes in contact with information sources appeared only with average total contacts—not categories of contact. Because of this broad contact with different types of information sources among all three jobtypes, academic librarians may be described as "generalists."

The conclusion that the academic librarian is a generalist regarding contact with types of information sources is interesting in light of research done by B. C. Vickery. He suggests three types of information use based on the following outcomes of work activity: (1) scientist—producing knowledge, (2) technician—creating functional designs, and (3) manager—generating decisions. Each implies a need for different types of information and involves different search strategies and information needs.

At one end of the continuum is the scientist with a narrow subject scan and a reliance on specific types of information. At the other end of the continuum is the manager or decision maker, who "will tend to be more of a generalist, faced by a variety of situations . . . with a relatively wide subject scan, [and] little time to devote to research."[7]

The data from this investigation combined with Vickery's analysis of information use suggest that academic librarians studied generally reflect information use characteristics described by Vickery as managerial. One might speculate that these information use characteristics suggest that academic librarians are more concerned with administrative matters relating to their specific responsibilities in the organization than to research, areas of specific topical interest, and individual production of knowledge. One might also speculate that these information use characteristics contribute to what some researchers have described as the general bureaucratic nature of academic librarians.[8]

A second conclusion that might be drawn from these results is that the degree of routineness associated with the jobtype is inversely related to each jobtype's number of contacts with information sources; that is, more contact with sources of information indicates a job with little routine. Recent research by Samuel Bacharach and Michael Aiken supports the hypothesis that employees who report their work as routine tend to engage in less communication activity than those employees who report their work as not routine.[9] If one considers contact with information sources as one form of communication activity, technical service librarians in this study may be described as involved in more routine work than other jobtypes in the academic library.

Similarly, if one assumes that contact with information sources resolves or reduces uncertainty, it may be suggested that the number of contacts with information sources is an indicator of the relative uncertainty associated with the performance of a given jobtype. Thus, the data suggest that administrators deal with more uncertainty (less routine) in the performance of their job than do public service librarians, who in turn deal with more uncertainty (less routine) than do technical service librarians. Thus, the bureaucratic nature of the academic librarian is more pronounced by the technical service librarians and public service librarians than by those dealing in administration.

An academic librarian's number of contacts with information sources may be a useful means to describe not only the jobtype's routineness but perhaps its other characteristics as well. Researchers in the area of organizational development and organizational communication may wish to examine more closely an employee's contact with types of information sources as they relate to specific jobtypes and other organizational characteristics. Additional variables such as managerial style and organizational climate also may be related to an employee's number of contacts with information sources.

In an academic library, an analysis of the number of information sources contacted by librarians appears to support what many librarians already suspect: technical service librarians engage in less overall information contact than do other members of the professional staff and, thus, deal with less uncertainty or more routine in the performance of their position than do other librarians. But, then, perhaps a number of positions in the academic library as currently constituted *require* limited contact with information sources for acceptable job performance. If this is true, occupants of such positions may be less academicians or scientists then technicians or technocrats.

NOTES

1. Abraham Kaplan, *The Conduct of Inquiry* (Scranton, Pa.: Chandler Publishing Company, 1964), pp. 184-85.

2. T. J. Allen, *Managing the Flow of Technology: Technology Transfer and the Dissemination of Technological Information Within the R & D Organization* (Cambridge, Mass.: MIT Press, 1977), pp. 63-65.

3. Lyman W. Porter and Karlene H. Roberts, "Communication in Organizations," in *Handbook of Industrial and Organizational Psychology,* ed. Martin D. Dunnette (Chicago: Rand McNally, 1976).

4. A. G. Smith, *Communication and Status: The Dynamics of a Research Center* (Eugene: University of Oregon, Center for the Advanced Study of Educational Administration, 1966).

5. *SPSS: Statistical Package for the Social Sciences,* 2nd ed. (New York: McGraw-Hill, 1975), p. 480.

6. William D. Wells and Jagdish N. Sheth, "Factor Analysis," in *Handbook of Marketing Research,* ed. Robert Ferber (New York: McGraw-Hill, 1974).

7. B. C. Vickery, *Information Systems* (Hamden, Conn.: Archon Books, 1973), pp. 47-48.

8. Kenneth H. Plate, *Management Personnel in Libraries: A Theoretical Model for Analysis* (Rockaway, N.J.: American Faculty Press, 1970).

9. Samuel Bacharach and Michael Aiken, "Communication in Administrative Bureaucracies," *Academy of Management Journal*, 20 (September 1977): 365-77.

5
POLITICAL IMPACT OF INFORMATION CONTACT

INTRODUCTION

In the previous chapter it was suggested that the concept of information potential might provide a useful framework to examine an individual's contact with and selection of information sources. Based on this concept it has been demonstrated that academic librarians differ substantially in the number of information sources they contact related to their job, organization, or profession. The question, however, that remains to be addressed is what effect does this information contact have on the individual's activity within the organization.

Before this question can be addressed, it may be useful to consider, briefly, information vis-à-vis the political process in the academic library. The political process may be defined in terms of the power relationships among organizational members. Individual political power, minimally, depends on the person's formal authority to enforce sanctions on other organizational members, the charismatic ability of the person to obtain recognition and interact effectively with other organizational members, and the person's ability to contact and select information sources of value to affect organizational decision making.

Within the formal organization, information is a basic resource in the political process because it converts into effective political power more readily than a number of other resources. More important, information resources do not follow the law of conservation of energy. They, unlike virtually any other resource, are not used up while being utilized. Furthermore, effective utilization of information resources enhances individual power within the organization through interaction rather than action.[1]

Effective control of information in the organization may also tend to enhance the power of the bureaucratic nature of the organization.[2] As previously pointed out, academic librarians tend to elicit information use characteristics that may be described as administrative. If the organization, or key individuals in the organization, can monopolize information selection, organization, storage, and retrieval, information resources can be manipulated to justify certain actions and decisions. Thus, the political power resulting from information control may be directly related to the ineffectiveness of organizational decision making.

An implication of such a relationship between information and the political process is that individuals may have a considerable degree of control over their involvement in the political process and thus decision making. Information, in itself, is neutral with respect to power. Only the individual can contact and select those information sources "necessary" to obtain power and thus affect the political process in the organization. As has been demonstrated in the previous chapter, an individual has a large degree of control in his or her contact with information sources. This is true in large part because access to some information sources is self-determined.

Norman Uphoff points out that technical and political information are two different items. Technical information pertains to methods of production and distribution of goods/services. Political information has to do with the intentions, ambitions, and capabilities of others who compete for power, authority, or preferred policies.[3] However, it is clear that an individual who wishes to modify the production and distribution of goods/services must first modify organizational policies.

The distinction between technical and political information is especially appropriate for librarians. Even more appropriate is understanding the relationship between the two. By and large, many librarians are concerned with what Uphoff has referred to as technical information. Such information allows the librarian to effectively produce certain outputs—be they answers to reference questions or production of catalog cards. Such a situation is not surprising in that for the vast majority of librarians, minimal contact with information sources will fulfill the day-to-day responsibilities of the job. In this sense, librarians may be called technicians.

On the other hand, librarians wishing to affect the political process within the organization may be described in terms of their contact with a greater number of information sources. For these individuals an understanding of the importance of contacting information for production as opposed to policy/power is evident. As Uphoff suggests, "technical information can have political consequences by enlarging power capabilities and political information can enlarge control over resources or improve their efficiency so that productive consequences ensue."[4] In short, each can enhance the other if the relationship is recognized and there is a desire to modify the policy/power structures in the organization.

In the case of academic librarians, contact with technical and political information sources may not be related so much to different sources as to total sources contacted. If such a proposition is true, one could expect a significant relationship between those librarians who contact substantial information sources and involvement in decision making. Such involvement may be considered as prima facie evidence of power within the political process. Figure 5-1 summarizes these relationships.

The political power of individual librarians can be examined on both a formal and informal basis. Formally, the director and the assistant/associate directors have responsibility for decision making in the academic library. Being involved in decision making means that for at least one specific decision situation both a director and a librarian agree that the librarian was consulted and provided informational input to the resolution of the decision situation. If the directors identify librarians who contact substantial information sources as being involved in decision making, support for the relationships as described in Figure 5-1 would be evident.

This figure is based on data presented in the preceding chapter. Thus, it should be remembered that *total* contacts with information sources appeared to be the primary difference among various jobtypes vis-à-vis contact with information sources. Little difference was noted as to contacts in terms of the four information categories summarized in Table 3-3. Thus, Figure 5-1 stresses *total* contacts with information sources.

On an informal basis, political power within the organization may come because a certain individual is sought for his or her opinions by a substantial number of other individuals. The person would have political power because his or her opinion regarding library operations receives more attention than the opinions of others. Such an individual may be described as an opinion leader. Based on previous discussions in this book, one might expect opinion leaders to contact substantially more information sources than other individuals in the organization if the relationships described in Figure 5-1 are accurate.

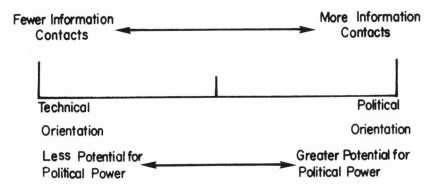

FIGURE 5-1   Relationship between Information Contact, Technical/Political Orientation, and Power within the Political Process

An examination of both the formal and the informal power relationships of librarians regarding contact with information sources is useful for the following reasons: first, it will help to explain the first component of information potential in terms of impact on the library political process; second, information as a resource, that is, a political resource, can be addressed in the reality of an organizational setting such as the academic library; third, the relationship between technical/political information can be explored in terms of the librarian's concern for and involvement in the organization's political process.

The question originally posed in this chapter was: what effect does information contact have on the individual's activity within the organization? To answer that question, a discussion of the relationship between contact with information sources, or information richness, and various types of librarian political categories will be presented. Three main categories are addressed: (1) information richness, composed of the information rich or the information poor, (2) involvement in decision making, composed of those involved in the decision making or political process and those not involved in the decision making or political process, and (3) sociometric type, composed of opinion leaders, participants, and isolates. The data for this discussion come from the information contact study previously described.

The discussion of the information richness, involvement in decision making, and sociometric type of academic librarians includes data on each group's social characteristics and type of information source contact. The chapter concludes with a brief discussion of the implications for information-rich and information-poor librarians within the context of political activity in the organization. Librarians wishing to modify the policies of the organization must be involved in the formal or informal political process. Contact with a substantial number of information sources appears to be a prerequisite for either kind of involvement.

INFORMATION RICHNESS AND DECISION MAKING

Information richness may be defined as the ability of certain individuals to come into contact with both more and better sources of information related to the individual's job, organization, or profession than other individuals in that organization. In order to determine which librarians in the study could be labeled as information rich or information poor, a procedure had to be developed to categorize the librarians.

Each librarian received a score to indicate contacts with information over a given period of time. Those librarians who ranked in the top fifty percent of contacts with information sources (see Table 3-3 for a list of these sources) were defined as information rich. Those who scored in the bottom forty-nine percent were defined as information poor. In each library investigated half of the librarians were categorized as information rich and half as information poor. Such a procedure assures that two groups will be identified based on contacts with information.

Table 5-1 describes the group characteristics of information-rich and information-poor librarians. In general, information-rich librarians tend to be male, better educated, and also administrators and public service librarians. However, the age, years of library employment, and years of professional experience of the information-rich librarians are similar to those of information-poor librarians.

TABLE 5-1

Group Characteristics of Information-
Rich and Information-Poor Librarians

	INFORMATION RICH (27)	INFORMATION POOR (29)
Sex (%)		
male	56	41
female	44	59
Average Age	40	43
Average Number of Years of Library		
Employment	8	8
Average Number of Years of Pro-		
fessional Experience	10	12
Education (%)**		
B.A.	6	3
M.L.S.	56	70
M.L.S.+*	33	24
Ph.D.	6	3
Average Number of Contacts with		
Sources of Information	78	31
Involved in Decision Making (%)		
yes	52	7
no	48	93
Jobtype (%)		
administrator	26	3
public service librarian	48	38
technical service librarian	26	59

*M.L.S.+ includes librarians with two or more subject master's degrees.
**Figures may not always total 100% due to rounding.

Of special interest is the likelihood of the information rich rather than
the information poor being involved in decision making. For information-
rich librarians, 52 percent are involved in decision making whereas only
7 percent of the information poor are. However, involvement in decision
making is not assured by being information rich.

The study also categorized librarians according to whether they were involved or not in decision making. If an administrator and a librarian agree that the librarian provided informational input to that administrator for at least one specific decision situation, the person is defined as involved in decision making. All other librarians are defined as not involved in decision making.

Table 5-2 describes the group characteristics of librarians involved in decision making, those not involved in decision making, and the information rich involved in decision making. The last category includes only librarians who were considered *both* involved in decision making and information rich. This figure highlights some of the differing characteristics between librarians who are involved in decision making and those who are not.

Decision making in these libraries is dominated by males, three-quarters of whom are involved in decision making. Furthermore, the educational background of those involved in decision making includes more formal education than for those not involved in decision making. And finally, it is apparent that administrators and public service librarians are more likely to be involved in decision making than technical service librarians. However, age, years of library employment, and years of professional experience are quite similar.

When librarians who are involved in decision making are compared to those who are information rich (see Table 5-1) a number of similarities appear. First, the average number of contacts with information sources is both high and similar. Second, administrators and public service librarians are more likely to be either information rich or involved in decision making than technical service librarians. However, librarians who are involved in decision making tend to have more formal education than information-rich librarians.

When examining the characteristics of the category "information rich involved in decision making" one notices, not surprisingly, their similarity to those who are involved in decision making. Of special interest is that average contacts with information increase over either the information-rich group or the involved-in-decision-making group. Clearly, the information rich involved in decision making are contacting a substantially larger number of information sources than the average librarian.

A closer examination of the information contacts for librarians involved and not involved in decision making is presented in Table 5-3. There are three main areas of differences between the two groups. First,

TABLE 5-2

Group Characteristics of Librarians Involved in
Decision Making, Not Involved in Decision Making,
and Information Rich Involved in Decision Making

	INVOLVED IN DECISION MAKING (16)	NOT INVOLVED IN DECISION MAKING (40)	INFORMATION RICH INVOLVED IN DECISION MAKING (12)
Sex (%)			
male	75	38	75
female	25	62	25
Average Age	41	42	40
Average Number of Years of Library Employment	9	8	9
Average Number of Years of Professional Experience	12	11	12
Education (%)			
B.A.	6	6	0
M.L.S.	38	72	40
M.L.S.+*	43	20	50
Ph.D.	13	2	10
Average Number of Contacts with Sources of Information	76	45	81
Jobtype (%)			
administrator	44	0	42
public service librarian	31	50	33
technical service librarian	25	50	25

*M.L.S.+ includes librarians with two or more subject master's degrees.

those involved belong to more than three university committees while those not involved belong to fewer than one. It should be stressed that university committees are external information sources since such information originates outside the library.

Second, librarians involved in decision making have substantially greater interpersonal contact than those not involved in decision making. As Table 5-3 demonstrates, those who are involved make more of *each type* of interpersonal contacts outside the library either through letters/ telephone calls or with others.

Finally, in terms of contact with the literature, either reading or writing, librarians who are involved in decision making read more articles, publish more book reviews, and participate in the writing of more internal reports/studies than librarians not involved in decision making. Indeed, from a case by case examination of individual librarians' contacts, the single best predictor of being involved in decision making appears to be participation in writing internal reports/studies.

The information contact characteristics of librarians involved in decision making might be described as an example of successfully thwarting the effects of bureaucracy frequently encountered in an academic library. In its attempt to control those situations in which interaction with the environment occurs, the bureaucratic form of organization has a tendency to isolate itself from the outside world and erect barriers to communication. Generally, it has been shown that in less complex, less formal, and more decentralized organizations, communication activity is greater than in a complex, formal, and centralized organization.[5]

The paradox appears to be that the larger and more formal the organization, the more difficult it is to contact outside information sources. But librarians who can successfully contact external sources of information are much more likely to be involved in the decision-making process and affect the political process. In this sense, librarians involved in decision making have not succumbed to the bureaucratic restraints apparently placed on information contact.

Although it is apparent that the information contacts of academic librarians categorized as information rich and involved in decision making differ from those of other librarians, the question remains, is there a significant relationship between information richness and involvement in decision making? To address this question, contingency tables describing the relationship between these two variables are presented in Figure 5-2.

TABLE 5-3

Average Number of Contacts with Information Sources by
Librarians Involved and Not Involved in Decision Making

	INVOLVED IN DECISION MAKING (16)	NOT INVOLVED IN DECISION MAKING (40)
1. Professional organizational membership	2.3	1.5
2. Professional organizational committee membership	1.0	.2
3. Professional meetings attended in last year	3.3	3.5
4. Papers, speeches, etc. presented at meetings during past year	.4	0
5. Elected positions in organizations at this time	1.8	.4
6. Membership in college/university committees	3.1	.6
7. Membership in library committees	1.6	.9
8. Memos per day to library organizational members	2.5	1.7
9. Letters or telephone calls per day made outside the library	6.6	3.9
10. Interpersonal contacts per day with library professionals	6.8	4.4
11. Interpersonal contacts per day with library paraprofessionals	4.6	2.7
12. Interpersonal contacts per day with faculty/administrators	3.1	2.7
13. Interpersonal contacts per day with others (vendors, etc.)	4.3	2.0
14. Size of personal collection	2.9	2.7
15. Journals currently subscribed to	2.4	1.5
16. Journals regularly scanned	5.2	4.5
17. Articles read per month	11.7	7.9
18. Articles published in last two years	.3	0
19. Book reviews published in last two years	3.5	.4
20. Books published in last two years	0	0
21. Internal studies/reports in last two years	8.6	2.5
22. Items being prepared for publication	.3	.2
AVERAGE TOTAL*	76	44

*Figures may not always equal total due to rounding.

LIBRARY A

	Involved in D-M	Not Involved in D-M	
Information Rich	5	2	7
Information Poor	0	8	8
	5	10	15

LIBRARY B

	Involved in D-M	Not Involved in D-M	
Information Rich	3	2	5
Information Poor	0	6	6
	3	8	11

LIBRARY C

	Involved in D-M	Not Involved in D-M	
Information Rich	3	5	8
Information Poor	1	7	8
	4	12	16

Relationship between information richness and involvement in decision making significant at .01 level*

*Combined significance level for independent tests

FIGURE 5-2   Relationship between Information Richness and Involvement in Decision Making

Before this figure is discussed, it should be noted that data from only three of the four libraries of the information contact study will be used in the presentation of contingency tables that represent relationships between various librarian types. Because a minor change was made on the pre-test by including an additional decision situation in Part III of the questionnaire, it is possible that any contingency tables from the pre-test would be invalid if compared to data from other libraries. To insure the integrity of the data presented in the following contingency tables, data from only libraries A, B, and C will be included.

In addition, the limitations of the contingency tables presented in this chapter must be recognized. The 2 X 2 tables were analyzed via Fisher's Exact Test, which is especially designed for such contingency tables and provides an accurate and somewhat conservative estimate of the significance of the relationships described. Other contingency tables in this chapter are 2 X 3 tables, which contain six cells. Since the number of professional librarians per library ranged between eleven and sixteen, the resultant cell sizes for a 2 X 3 contingency table are quite small. Fisher's Exact Test can be used only for 2 X 2 contingency tables; therefore, a chi-square test must be used on the 2 X 3 tables. A chi-square analysis of contingency tables with fewer than five cases per cell produces significance levels that should be viewed only as tentative.[6]

To compute the level of significance of the relationships in Figure 5-2 a chi-square test was performed on each contingency table. It should be noted that *Statistical Package for the Social Sciences* computes Fisher's Exact Test in place of a Pearson chi-square for 2 X 2 contingency tables. In reality, Fisher's Exact Test is an exact test for a 2 X 2 contingency table and may be used with very small samples,[7] for which it provides a more accurate approximation of the relationship between two variables. For libraries A, B, and C the relationship between organizational information richness and involvement in decision making is significant at the .006, the .06, and the .28 levels, respectively.

To obtain a level of significance of the relationship between these variables for all three libraries, it is necessary to utilize a procedure that can combine scores of independent tests. A chi-square can be computed for three independent tests based on the following formula:[8]

$X2 = -2$ (log p1 + log p2 + log p3) where:
1. $X2$ = chi-square
2. log p1 = log of probability 1 (.006)

3. log p2 = log of probability 2 (.06)
4. log p3 = log of probability 3 (.28)

The degrees of freedom equal two times the number of independent tests or, in this instance, six. Thus, using the above procedure, a combined test of the relationship between organizational information richness and involvement in decision making produces a chi-square of 18.4 with six degrees of freedom, which is significant at the .01 level.

An examination of Figure 5-2 clearly indicates the relationship between information richness and involvement in decision making. By inspection, it is evident that of the twelve librarians categorized as involved in decision making, eleven also are information rich. Looking at the bottom left cell in each contingency table, one notices that it is extremely unlikely for a librarian to be information poor and also be involved in decision making.

These contingency tables also suggest that it is *necessary* but not *sufficient* for an individual to be information rich if he or she is also to be involved in decision making. This conclusion is evident since 50 percent of those persons identified as information rich also were involved in decision making. It may be suggested that the information contact characteristics of information rich who are involved in decision making are different from those of the information rich not involved in decision making.

A case by case examination of the differences between these two groups suggests that presence of information contact emphasizing the following sources/situations predicts that the information rich will also be involved in decision making:

1. attending university/college committees
2. engaging in interpersonal contact of all types, especially external sources
3. publishing book reviews
4. participating in internal studies/reports

Although increased contact with information sources/situations is necessary to be labeled as information rich, information-rich librarians who tend to emphasize contact with the above four types of sources/situations are those who tend also to be involved in decision making.

In the previous chapter the number of contacts with information sources/situations for each librarian jobtype was found to have been significantly different. Figure 5-3 presents contingency tables relating jobtype and information richness. A chi-square analysis shows that for libraries A, B, and C the relationship between jobtype and information richness is significant at the .06, the .38, and the .10 levels, respectively. Using the technique previously described in this chapter to combine scores of independent tests, a combined test of the relationship between information richness and jobtype produces a chi-square of 12.1 with six degrees of freedom that is significant at the .08 level. However, the small cell sizes in these contingency tables make the findings tentative.

This significance level suggests that there is a relationship between information richness and jobtype. An inspection of the contingency tables in this figure suggests that administrators will tend to be information rich, public service librarians have an equal likelihood of being either information rich or information poor, and technical service librarians tend to be information poor. Keeping in mind that information richness, as defined in this investigation, is a measure of contacts with selected information sources, support is given to the idea that the jobtype may be an important determinant of the relative information richness of an academic librarian. Furthermore, in each of these contingency tables, one should note that the top right cell, administrators who are information poor, is zero; to be an administrator is to be information rich.

The concept of information richness appears to provide some explanation of the librarian's involvement in the political process. A significant relationship exists between involvement in decision making and information richness. Information richness appears to be necessary but not sufficient for involvement in decision making. However, if only those information-rich librarians who emphasize contact with university/college committees, interpersonal contacts, book reviews, and participation in internal studies/reports are considered, involvement in decision making tends to increase significantly. All administrators were found to be information rich, which suggests that they have better control over various bureaucratic restraints on organizational communication activity. And, finally, the political process clearly appears to be affected most by those librarians who contact substantial information sources.

INFORMATION SEEKING AND OPINION LEADERS

A second means of examining the political process in an academic library is to describe the informal patterns of information seeking, that is, which librarians are sought for their advice, information, or analysis of issues related to the organization. The information-seeking types within the communication network will help to explain the relationship of information source contact and the informal political process. Furthermore, such a technique may identify opinion leaders, or gatekeepers, within the information-seeking network of the library.

The study of the information-seeking networks will be based on previous work done by Nan Lin.[9] Lin has described member components of communication networks in his work. Those definitions have been modified to reflect the relatively small sizes of the networks being examined in this study and to make the terminology consistent with other terms previously used in the study. The definitions to be used are:

1. *Opinion Leader*—A person who is nominated by at least two other individuals in a group as the primary person he or she would go to for information.
2. *Participant*—A person who is not nominated by two or more group members but does seek information from another individual in the group.
3. *Isolate*—A person who does not seek information from another member of the group.

In reality, these definitions are more stringent (given the size of library groups being studied) than the definitions suggested by Lin. Based on these definitions, opinion leaders, participants, and isolates can be identified and the information contact of opinion leaders can be compared to other librarian types as well as to "gatekeepers," as is suggested by T. J. Allen.[10]

All fifty-six subjects in the four libraries responded to this question: Please name one person on whom you most frequently rely to obtain information about general operations or conditions in the library. The question forces the respondent to give one and only one name of another member of the organization. In every case, for those librarians who named another individual, the person named was a professional librarian and not a paraprofessional, student, or other type of organizational member. The information-seeking network for each library is presented in Figures 5-4 through 5-7.

LIBRARY A

	Information Rich	Information Poor	
Administrator	3	0	3
Public Services Librarian	3	3	6
Technical Services Librarian	1	5	6
	7	8	15

LIBRARY B

	Information Rich	Information Poor	
Administrator	1	0	1
Public Services Librarian	3	3	6
Technical Services Librarian	1	3	4
	5	6	11

LIBRARY C

	Information Rich	Information Poor	
Administrator	2	0	2
Public Services Librarian	3	1	4
Technical Services Librarian	3	7	10
	8	9	16

Relationship between information richness and librarian jobtype significant at .08 level*

*Combined significance level for independent tests

FIGURE 5-3   Relationship between Information Richness and Librarian Jobtype

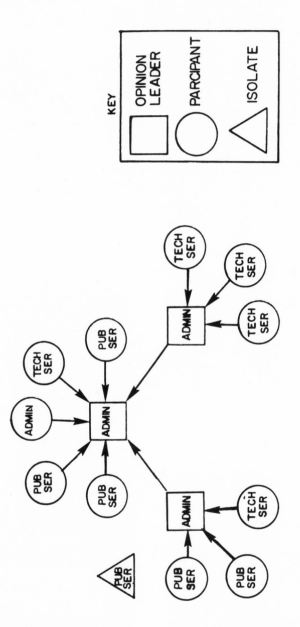

KEY

☐ OPINION LEADER

◯ PARCIPANT

△ ISOLATE

FIGURE 5-4 Information Seeking Network Library A

104

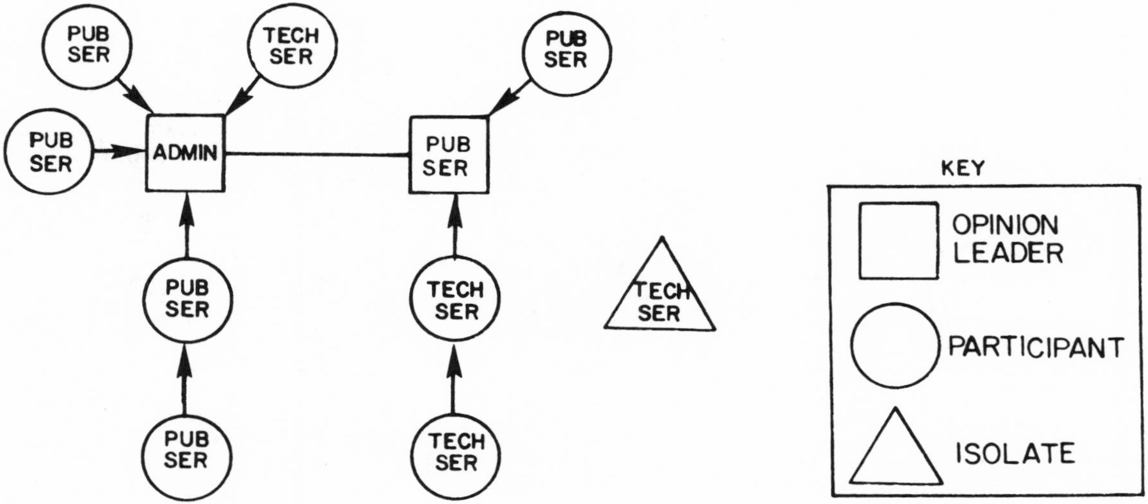

KEY

☐ OPINION LEADER

◯ PARTICIPANT

△ ISOLATE

FIGURE 5-5 Information Seeking Network Library B

105

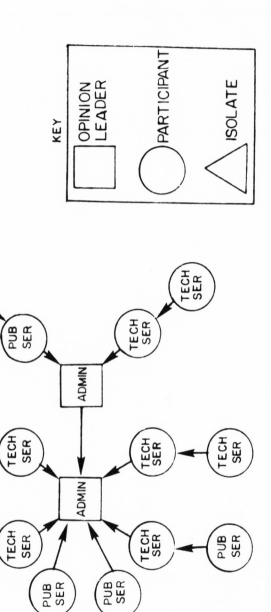

FIGURE 5-6 Information Seeking Network Library C

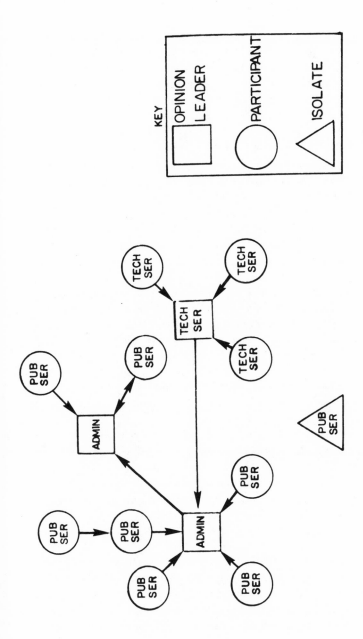

FIGURE 5-7 Information Seeking Network Library D

107

An inspection of Figures 5-4 through 5-7 indicates that there are two opinion leaders for libraries B and C and three opinion leaders for libraries A and D. Additionally, it will be noticed that the technical service librarians tend to seek information from different opinion leaders than the public service librarians. Only three isolates were identified, two public service librarians and one technical service librarian.

Although individual organization charts for each library cannot be presented if the confidentiality of the libraries involved in the study is to be maintained, it may be said that the information-seeking networks almost invariably follow the formal authority lines of the organization. For instance, public service librarians seek information from the associate director for public service and technical service librarians seek information from the associate director for technical services. In short, the information-seeking networks are abbreviated sociometric diagrams of the formal organization charts.

Communication network researchers such as Roberts and O'Reilly have suggested that an organization has both an authority communication network (one which details the responsibility and authority relationships among the various members of the organization) and an expertise network (one which explains specific tasks such as "how-to-do-it" or "how-to-improve-it" or where to obtain relevant information about some problem).[11] The information-seeking networks diagramed in Figures 5-4 through 5-7 more closely fit their description of the authority network than the expertise network since they follow the formal communication patterns suggested by the organization chart.

The information-seeking networks clearly identify opinion leaders in each library. All told, ten opinion leaders are identified from the four libraries studied. The characteristics of this group of librarians are summarized in Table 5-4. A comparison of the characteristics of opinion leaders with other librarian groups represented in Tables 5-1 and 5-2 shows similarities between opinion leaders and the information-rich group, as well as between opinion leaders and those involved in decision making.

Compared to other librarians, opinion leaders tend to be male, they have more years of professional experience, are better educated, are involved in decision making, and tend to be administrators. Most striking is the fact that 100 percent of the opinion leaders are involved in decision making. This factor is more significant because opinion leaders were

TABLE 5-4

Group Characteristics of Opinion Leaders

	OPINION LEADERS (10)
Sex (%)	
male	80
female	20
Average Age	43
Average Number of Years of Library Employment	10
Average Number of Years of Professional Experience	13
Education (%)	
B.A.	0
M.L.S.	40
M.L.S.+*	50
Ph.D.	10
Average Number of Factual Sources of Information	77
Involved in Decision Making (%)	
yes	100
no	0
Jobtype (%)	
administrator	70
public service librarian	10
technical service librarian	20

*M.L.S.+ includes librarians with two or more subject master's degrees.

selected by colleagues on an informal basis. Clearly, other librarians in these libraries know to contact people likely to be well-informed to obtain information.

Previously, it was pointed out that being information rich was necessary but not sufficient to be involved in decision making. Because the sociometric analysis of information seeking indicates that all opinion leaders are involved in decision making, it is useful to compare the information contacts of the two groups. Table 5-5 presents average number of contacts with information sources for both information-rich librarians and opinion leaders.

TABLE 5-5

Average Number of Contacts with Information Sources by
Information-Rich Librarians and Opinion Leaders

	INFORMATION RICH (27)	OPINION LEADER (10)
1. Professional organizational membership	2.4	2.3
2. Professional organizational committee membership	.8	1.1
3. Professional meetings attended in last year	4.5	2.3
4. Papers, speeches, etc. presented at meetings during past year	.3	.4
5. Elected positions in organizations at this time	1.0	1.2
6. Membership in college/university committees	2.4	4.1
7. Membership in library committees	1.4	1.8
8. Memos per day to library organizational members	2.8	2.5
9. Letters or telephone calls per day made outside the library	8.8	5.5
10. Interpersonal contacts per day with library professionals	6.5	7.5
11. Interpersonal contacts per day with library paraprofessionals	4.4	5.2
12. Interpersonal contacts per day with faculty/administrators	4.7	4.0
13. Interpersonal contacts per day with others (vendors, etc.)	4.7	4.8
14. Size of personal collection	3.2	2.4
15. Journals currently subscribed to	2.6	2.2
16. Journals regularly scanned	6.0	5.4
17. Articles read per month	12.7	11.2
18. Articles published in last two years	.1	.2
19. Book reviews published in last two years	2.6	2.8
20. Books published in last two years	0	0
21. Internal studies/reports in last two years	6.1	11.0
22. Items being prepared for publication	.2	.5
AVERAGE TOTAL*	78	77

*Figures may not always equal the total due to rounding.

In general, it may be said that information contacts for these two groups are quite similar. However, the few differences between them are most interesting. Although information rich librarians attend more professional meetings, opinion leaders have substantially more involvement in university/college committees. Also of interest is that information-rich librarians tend to emphasize external interpersonal contact whereas opinion leaders tend to emphasize internal interpersonal contact. The most significant difference is that opinion leaders have much more involvement in internal reports/studies than do the information rich.

The difference between information-rich librarians and opinion leaders is interesting in light of recent findings by T. J. Allen. He has examined the organizational role of the information officer and gatekeeper in a research and development organization. The information contact characteristics of the information-rich librarian closely follow those of the information officer while those of the opinion leader closely resemble the characteristics of the gatekeeper.

Allen's major point is that the information officer (information rich) and the gatekeeper (opinion leader) serve different communication purposes. "The gatekeeper may not be as knowledgeable about the various sources of information, but he does know far more of their content than the information officer does. In other words, while an information officer provides range, the gatekeeper provides depth."[12] Thus, the information roles of the two in an organization are not competitive but rather complementary. Allen's analysis appears to match the information contact characteristics and roles of the information-rich librarians and opinion leaders found in this study.

Another method to analyze the characteristics of the opinion leader is to examine the relationship between sociometric type and involvement in decision making. Figure 5-8 presents contingency tables describing this relationship at libraries A, B, and C. An inspection of these contingency tables shows that all opinion leaders in libraries A, B, and C are involved in decision making. A chi-square analysis shows that for libraries A, B, and C, the relationship between sociometric type and involvement in decision making is significant at the .02, the .03, and the .05 levels, respectively. Using the technique previously described in this chapter to combine scores of independent tests, a combined test of the relationship between sociometric type and involvement in decision making produces a chi-square of 20.8 with six degrees of freedom which is significant at the .01 level.

Library A

	Involved in D-M	Not Involved in D-M	
Opinion Leader	3	0	3
Participant	2	9	11
Isolate	0	1	1
	5	10	15

Library B

	Involved in D-M	Not Involved in D-M	
Opinion Leader	2	1	2
Participant	1	7	8
Isolate	0	1	1
	3	8	11

Library C*

	Involved in D-M	Not Involved in D-M	
Opinion Leader	2	0	2
Participant	2	12	14
	4	12	14

Relationship between involvement in
decision making and sociometric type
significant at .01 level.‡

*A 2x2 contingency table has been computed instead of a 2x3 contingency table
because no isolates were identified at Library C.

‡Combined significance level for independent tests

FIGURE 5-8 Relationship between Involvement in Decision Making and Sociometric Type

Keeping in mind that involvement in decision making was determined by agreement between administrator and the librarian as to the librarian's informational input vis-à-vis a specific decision situation, these contingency tables reflect the administrator's preference to involve opinion leaders in the decision-making process. Because opinion leaders also tend to be information rich, additional support is provided for the proposition that those people who are identified as organizational information rich will tend to be involved in decision making.

It is also interesting to note that the relationship between sociometric type and involvement in decision making (significant at the .01 level) is stronger than the relationship between sociometric type and information richness (significant at the .10 level). The comparison between these two relationships suggests that the selection of opinion leaders is related to individual involvement in decision making rather than to the large quantity of contacts with information sources. Such an analysis tends to support the ideas of T. J. Allen regarding the different roles of information rich and the opinion leaders. Although both may affect the political process in the library, they may do so in different ways.

Allen has suggested that gatekeepers in the research and development setting tend to be better educated, first line supervisors, more likely to be selected for special task forces within their organization as well as the profession, similar to their colleagues in age, but, above all, high performers and extremely competent. All of these characteristics describe the opinion leaders identified in this study.[13]

Although data were not collected in this study to address other characteristics, it may be suggested that opinion leaders in these libraries demonstrate additional characteristics described by Allen's gatekeepers: they tend to prefer working with a number of people and sharing responsibility for projects; they prefer to distribute their time somewhat over a number of activities to investing it primarily in a single project; and they devote a significantly larger portion of their time to administrative activities.[14] With such information contact and other social characteristics, opinion leaders play a significant role in the library political process.

Sociometric analysis identifies communication roles within an organization and provides a basis for describing network activity in terms of generalized role characteristics. Research in this area is relatively limited. However, Roberts and O'Reilly suggest that personality traits such as self-assurance, status needs, motivational variables, and demographic characteristics may predict role stability over time.[15] Regardless of the research methodology employed in communication network analysis, these researchers conclude that "overall, the picture is one of dysfunctional aspects for individuals who are not integrated into organizational communication networks."[16]

CONTACT WITH INFORMATION AS A POLITICAL RESOURCE

An examination of contact with information in both the formal and informal political process suggests that some librarians are much more adept at affecting the political process. Significantly, those librarians who do affect the political process have greater contact with various types of information sources. For these librarians, the importance of information as a political resource has been recognized. Furthermore, their information-handling expertise, expecially in the case of opinion leaders, is easily identified by administrators and colleagues.

The broad range of information contacts for various types of librarians is represented in Table 5-6. The average librarian who participated in this study came into contact with fifty-four information sources. But, it is evident that average contact with information does not increase the probability of affecting the political process. To be involved in decision making, either on an informal or formal basis, having above average contact with information sources is a prerequisite.

Within the organization, information contact must be considered a key component of the political process. Politics encompasses those activities and attitudes that affect the acquisition and/or exercise of authority as vested in specialized functional roles and expressed as power.[17] A specific communication role, such as an opinion leader, is an excellent example of a power base within the library organization that can be used to affect policies, production, and services. Their 100 percent involvement in decision making is prima facie evidence of their ability to affect decisions. Their contact with information may be characterized as politically motivated—that is, it pertains to the organizational policies in a broad sense.

Norman Uphoff's differentiation of political and technical information appears to be a useful basis from which an overview can be developed to describe a librarian's information-handling ability. Uphoff suggested that technical information contact is closely related to production of goods and services, whereas political information is closely related to the exercise of authority and power. However, this concept does not consider those people who might be termed reclusive—having virtually no information contact—or zealot—having excessive or overabundant contact with information. The recluse, technician, politician, and zealot can be described both in terms of purpose of information contact and quantity of contact.

TABLE 5-6

Average Contacts with Information Sources by Type of Librarian*

LIBRARIAN TYPE	AVERAGE CONTACTS
Administrators	90
Information Rich Involved in Decision Making	81
Information Rich	78
Opinion Leaders	77
Involved in Decision Making	76
Public Service Librarians	54
All Librarians	54
Not Involved in Decision Making	45
Technical Service Librarians	40
Information Poor	31

*Membership in these groups is not mutually exclusive. These groupings represent all groups for which individual analysis was done.

The recluse sees no purpose in making an effort to contact his or her information environment. During the interviews librarians who said, "I have little or no need to contact these information sources [on the list]," or "I don't need information from anyone in order to do my job," appear to fit this category of information recluse. Not only do they contact very few sources of information, they also see themselves as outside any need for such contact. Furthermore, most had no desire to be active in the organization's political process or to be involved in decision making.

Technicians probably compose the majority of librarians as described by their information-handling ability. Their contact with information sources typically is average or below. But of equal importance is the consideration that the purpose of contact with information sources is limited to their product or service. During interviews, these people appeared to be concerned mainly with information sources that enabled them to do an adequate job. Once they believed their performance was "adequate" in producing a specific product or service, their need for information contact was satisfied. However, a number of technicians wanted to be involved in organizational decision making but appeared to be frustrated by their exclusion from the process.

The politician differs from the technician in two important areas. First, the purpose of his or her contact with information is to affect policies at an organizational level as well as to maintain at least "adequate" performance for his or her specific areas of responsibility. Because of the desire to affect organizational policies the person contacts substantially larger numbers of information sources than other librarians. During the interviews, politicians became evident because of their concern for contacting information that pertained to broad areas of the library or to issues currently affecting the profession. Interestingly, many of these librarians who were involved in decision making or were opinion leaders were not aware of their status although library administrators usually could identify them as such.

Librarians also can be categorized as zealots according to their contact with information. Zealots fail to identify which sources need not be contacted; therefore, they try to contact all types of information sources in excessive quantity. Their purpose for contacting various sources is unclear. Typically, they have a broad range of interests and many types of information compete for their attention. In this study, two participants contacted an average of 150 information sources, which is almost three times that of the average librarian. Although both can be categorized as information rich, neither was involved in decision making and neither was an opinion leader. Their lack of discrimination in their contact with information limits their ability to affect the political process.

Thus, it can be suggested that these categories of librarians, based on number of contacts and purpose of contact, can be related to affecting the library's political process. This relationship is described in Figure 5-9. As such, it is a refinement of Figure 5-1 since it accommodates those people who contact little to no information as well as those who are contacting too much information indiscriminately. Figure 5-9 presents a general view relating information contact with political activity,

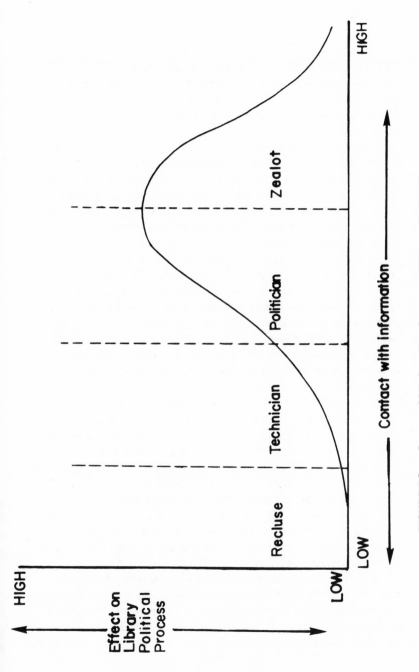

FIGURE 5-9   Contact with Information Sources and Effect on Political Process

indicating *necessary* conditions which in themselves may not be sufficient for involvement in the political process. Personality characteristics, among a broad range of other variables, may also be related to involvement in the library political process. However, information-handling ability is likely to be a prerequisite for affecting political processes.

The two extremes of the curve, the recluse and the zealot, appear to include no more than 10 percent each in the libraries studied. By and large most librarians fall into the category described as technicians: they contact only enough information to perform their job at an acceptable level of performance. Librarians are largely uninformed about organizational concerns that affect other library departments, national issues of concern to information professionals, and the impact of various types of new technology on the library environment.

A concept that may be described as optimal ignorance is useful to describe the typical situation. Optimal ignorance is based on the idea that *not* knowing certain things may in fact be beneficial for the individual. Uphoff contends that persons concerned with information are likely to overestimate benefits from additional information and to underestimate the costs incurred in acquiring it.[18] While this may be true for researchers, optimal ignorance for academic librarians implies that their ignorance is related to organizational matters and not to their specific department or job responsibilities.

During the interview sessions a large number of librarians went out of their way to rationalize their limited contact with information sources. For some, the need to learn or to stay abreast of new developments was ignored. Yet, they maintained enough contact with information sources to insure, in their opinion, adequate job performance. They accepted the idea of not knowing certain things or not contacting certain types of information—likely as not because such action was not encouraged or few rewards were provided for such behavior. Furthermore, a contributing factor to optimal ignorance is that the librarians perceive little uncertainty with their responsibilities and therefore there is little need for contacting information.

The notion of optimal ignorance is applied here in a much different manner from that used by Uphoff. He would apply the term to the zealots who need first to identify what it is they need to know rather than to contact all information possible. Information overload is not a problem for the average librarian; indeed the opposite is more likely. Because many librarians contact relatively few sources that have little direct bearing on organizational matters, they find themselves outside the political or decision-making process.

A final consideration that contributes to optimal ignorance is that information is likely to be more productive for those individuals who have other resources, such as time, status, and financial control in the organization. Because informaion, in itself, is neutral as to power, its effectiveness as a resource depends on how well an individual can utilize it as a catalyst with additional resources. Most of the librarians in this study had virtually no free time because they were consumed by daily chores; they had limited status in the library and less in the university; and their financial control went only as far, maybe, as the book budget. In short, many academic librarians have little or no control over other resources which, when combined with information, might allow them to affect the political process.

Nonetheless, the concepts of information richness and opinion leaders are important to understand contact with information and the political process in the library. The concept of information richness helps to explain organizational information handling. M. C. Yovits has provided a general model for the analysis and flow of information, which is reproduced in Figure 5-10.[19] In the formal organization it may be suggested that it is this person—this information-rich person—who provides the link between information acquisition/dissemination and decision making. This link is between both the organization and the outside environment (as an information-rich employee) or among the various component members of the library (as an opinion leader). Both roles contribute to effective organization information handling.

Both the information-rich employee and the opinion leader must acquire, process, and disseminate information to be of organizational value. All three components must be present, as depicted in Figure 5-11, for improved organizational information handling. For an employee to merely acquire and access more relevant information than his fellow workers is of minimal benefit to the organization as a whole unless that information is also processed into organizational information needs and disseminated to those people in the organization to whom the information is more relevant and needed.

The three components can be briefly defined. "Acquires information" can be seen as a quantitative number of information sources with

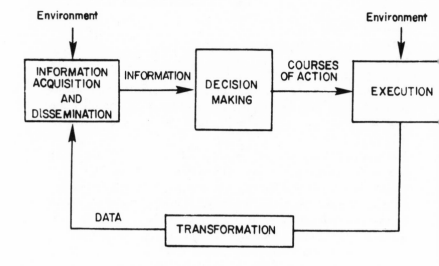

FIGURE 5-10   Analysis and Flow of Information

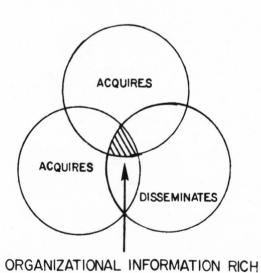

ORGANIZATIONAL INFORMATION RICH

FIGURE 5-11   The Concept of Organizational Information Rich

which the person comes into contact. "Processes information" is a qualitative component in which the person's innate ability to organize information through analysis/synthesis matches that information with the information needs of the organization. "Disseminates information" is the active component and determines the number of communication contacts of the person by either making him- or herself available or actively providing the structured information to other individuals at the appropriate time.

Merely possessing "more" or "better" information than other organization members does not automatically mean that such organizational information rich are actively contributing to the making of the decisions in that organization. Nor can one assume that the information held by an information-rich employee is recognized as a valuable resource by the organization and, specifically, top management. However, the notion that "better" decisions would result if the organizational information rich were involved in the decision-making process does seem to warrant investigation. In fact, the crux of the matter is to determine whether administrators utilize information-rich employees and opinion leaders during the decision-making process and for disseminating information throughout the organization, and make other resources available to these special individuals so that they can better utilize their increased information potential.

Indeed, the whole concept of employee evaluation and performance measures in terms of information-handling ability—sources of information with which the person comes into contact and ability to select additional sources for specific decision situations—might drastically improve the productivity of the organization whether it be product or service oriented. Traditional evaluation methods either of basic personality characteristics or ability to accomplish predetermined goals may be ignoring a prime determinant to organizational effectiveness when information activity is not considered.

The complexity of decision making in most academic libraries demands that administrators utilize *all* resources toward improved decisions. Two important resources are information and the individual employee. Of these two, the best resource is that individual who has high information potential based on contacts with information. A number of bureaucratic restraints can limit an individual's ability to affect the organizational political process. However, administrators and all other librarians must learn how to examine their contact with information sources, to identify the information rich and opinion leaders, and to utilize these individuals in the decision-making process. It may be suggested that through such individuals other scarce resources, such as time, personnel, money, and equipment, can be better utilized to better accomplish organizational goals and objectives.

NOTES

1. Theodore Lowi, "Government and Politics: Blurring of Sector Lines, Rise of New Elites," in *Information Technology: Some Critical Implications for Decision Makers* (New York: The Conference Board, 1972), pp. 136-37.

2. W. T. Durr, "Information as a Source of Bureaucratic Power in the Political Decision Making Process," in *The Information Age in Perspective: Proceedings of the ASIS Annual Meeting,* Vol. 15, Comp. Everett H. Brenner (White Plains, N.Y.: Knowledge Industries, 1978), pp. 119-22,

3. Norman Thomas Uphoff, "Information as a Political Resource," in *Humanization of Knowledge in the Social Sciences,* ed. Pauline Atherton (Syracuse: Syracuse University, School of Library Science, 1972), p. 44.

4. Ibid., pp. 44-45.

5. J. Haige, M. Aiken, and C. B. Marrett, "Organization Structure and Communications," *American Sociological Review,* 36 (1971): 860-71.

6. Herman J. Leother and Donald G. McTavish, *Inferential Statistics for Sociologists* (Boston: Allyn and Bacon, 1974), p. 219.

7. John T. Roscoe, *Fundamental Research Statistics for the Behavioral Sciences,* 2nd ed. (New York: Holt, Rinehart and Winston, 1975), pp. 281-85.

8. Ramon C. Littell and J. Leroy Folks, "Asymptotic Optimality of Fisher's Method of Combining Independent Tests," *Journal of the American Statistical Association,* 66 (December 1971): 803.

9. Nan Lin, *Foundations of Social Research* (New York: McGraw-Hill, 1976), pp. 329-33.

10. T. J. Allen, *Managing the Flow of Technology: Technology Transfer and the Dissemination of Technological Information Within the R & D Organization* (Cambridge: The M.I.T. Press, 1977), pp. 165-68.

11. Karlene H. Roberts and Charles R. O'Reilly, III, *Organizations as Communication Structures: An Empirical-Theoretical Approach* (Berkeley: University of California, Institute of Industrial Relations, 1975), NTIS Document No. AD-A013 675/4GA.

12. Allen, *Managing the Flow of Technology,* p. 166.

13. Ibid., pp. 163-80.

14. Ibid., p. 180.

15. Karlene H. Roberts and Charles A. O'Reilly, III, "Organizations as Communication Structures: An Empirical Approach," *Human Communication Research,* 4 (Summer 1978): 290-91.

16. Karlene H. Roberts and Charles A. O'Reilly, III, "Some Correlations of Communication Roles in Organizations," *Academy of Management Journal,* 22 (March 1979): 54.

17. Warren F. Ilchman and Norman Thomas Uphoff, *The Political Economy of Change* (Berkeley: University of California Press, 1969), pp. 50-51 and 73-89.

18. Uphoff, "Information as a Political Resource," p. 50.

19. Bruce J. Whittemore and M. C. Yovits, "A Generalized Conceptual Development for the Analysis and Flow of Information," *Journal of the American Society for Information Science,* 24 (May-June 1973): 221-31.

6

PERCEIVED VALUE
OF INFORMATION SOURCES FOR
LIBRARY DECISION SITUATIONS

EVALUATION OF INFORMATION SOURCES

This volume has suggested that a person's information potential is composed of two primary components: (1) the person's contact with information sources, and (2) the ability to select appropriate information sources to resolve specific decision situations. This chapter examines an individual's information-handling ability at a very specific level. On a daily basis, organizational members may be forced to make decisions affecting a broad range of topics. In order to make such decisions they may wish to obtain information from any of a number of possible sources. Based on a number of value preferences, the individual will select an information source that he or she perceives as likely to help resolve a specific decision situation.

A primary question that might be asked is, "What information sources do professional librarians select as their first choice to resolve a specific library decision situation?" Answers to this question would provide a basis for estimating perceived values of various types of information sources for specific decision situations. Knowing *what* sources are perceived as valuable is an important first research step that may provide some direction in determining *why* sources are selected.

Evaluation of information sources suggests that an individual consciously identifies criteria by which the relative worth or importance of the source is anticipated for a specific decision situation. This process of evaluation is related to a myriad of personal and environmental factors for each individual. Indeed, the study of human values is probably one of the most complex fields of scientific inquiry.[1] But, basic value preferences of an individual may affect the selection of an information source.

Despite the complexities of this topic, some assumptions can be made about perceived value of information sources for specific decision situations. From general systems theory, notions of purposefulness, feedback, and differentiation are important considerations. In the process of obtaining information for a specific decision, it is assumed that the seeker of that information is teleological or purposeful. His or her goal may be implicit in the sense of wanting to resolve the decision situation or wanting to obtain "use-ful" information.

Human information processing systems appear to be governed on a long-term basis by feedback. Because of feedback on the usefulness of an information source for specific situations, future behavior is modified or regulated. This ongoing evaluation and feedback allows the system (person) to correct the differences between actual and intended results. However, for feedback to be useful in this regulation process, there must be an inner reference system of values, criteria, or guidelines. Based on such a system there is constant comparison, testing, and monitoring of current performance. "In effect, the system is comparing the existing state [of the information] to a desired or intended state."[2]

Related to the feedback process is differentiation, that is, replacement of general patterns by more specialized functions. When information sources are evaluated they are divided into certain categories and types. As in this study, information sources have been described for academic librarians in twenty specific categories. Even within these categories, information sources may be further differentiated by certain criteria. This differentiation process is a direct result of the monitoring of actual results from a selected information source compared to a desired result.

A key word in the discussion of the evaluation of information sources for specific decision situations is "relative." Two people may evaluate the appropriateness of an information source for a specific decision situation entirely differently. The personal values, past experiences, and perceived benefits of a source are likely to be different for each person. Furthermore, a source that is perceived as valuable by one person, because of these factors, may not be valuable for another who brings a different gestalt to the situation. In short, perceived value of information sources represents an ongoing historical perception of the *relative* usefulness of an information source within the systems framework previously described.

Although it is not the purpose of this section to provide an in-depth analysis of the concept of perceived value of an information source for decision making, a brief discussion of the concept in broad terms does appear to be necessary. When an individual selects an information source for decision making, that selection typically is made *before* an actual examination of the specific source is possible. Therefore, the decision to select a certain information source is a perceived evaluation of the probable or expected value of a specific source.

Thus, the perceived value is a broad concept that includes a number of components all related to each other by the person's inner value system. A general theoretical stance that might be useful to explain perceived value of an information source for a specific decision situation is:

Perceived Value = f (Non-Utilities) + (Utilities) where: f = Function of individual's value system, with examples of Non-Utilities such as:

1. accuracy of information source
2. expected benefits of selecting source
3. cost of the source

and Utilities such as:

1. format
2. form
3. timeliness
4. physical availability

This model is suggested as a heuristic to aid in our conceptualization of the perceived value of information. Based on such a model we might better understand the nature of the data that are presented in this chapter as well as provide a basis for speculation on the implications of the data.

This model suggests that perceived value is a function of two general sets of variables: non-utility, directly related to the *content* of the information, and utility, which are *not* related to the content of the information. The combination of these variables, as a function of the individual's value system, provides a general model to examine the concept of perceived value of information for decision making.

In such a model it may be suggested that different individuals may, in effect, weigh the importance of one variable over another. As yet, little research has been done to understand this phenomenon. However, utility and non-utility preferences appear to be gaining some respectability as a heuristic to study the value of information.[3] At a conceptual level, comparison of those concepts may provide a means to identify preferences and also suggest techniques by which preferences can be shaped or modified for certain situations, such as the selection of information sources!

Implicit in the selection of an information source is accuracy; on a deductive basis, the perceived value of an information source should be related to its perceived accurateness. Similarly with cost, one might assume that there is a break-even point whereupon the value of the information no longer equals its expected cost. Furthermore, that cost may be described in psychological terms as well as traditional economic terms. An information source (such as another person) may not be selected if the cost in lost status or embarrassment is too high. The third non-utility variable is expected benefits. Selection of an information source may depend, in part, on the perceived benefits that may result from selecting one source rather than another. Such benefits may take the shape of power—either personal, social, or political; status in the organization or profession; recognition for using a specific source rather than another; or a host of other benefits such as time saved. Clearly these three variables would appear to play an important role in the decision to select one information source rather than another.

Because of the complexity of values, evaluation, and perceived versus actual value, the concept of utilities has been suggested an an approach to information evaluation. Utilities are characteristics or aspects of a product or service that explain their worth or value. As such they are criteria, or indicators by which an information source can be judged and compared against another information source. Utility concepts allow the researcher to better understand "how the nature of information, *exclusive of its content,* may facilitate or retard its use and value"[4] (author's emphasis). A number of information utilities may be identified as a basis for determining the value of an information source for academic librarians. Although more utilities may be identified, the four appear to be especially important and have been incorporated in the conceptual basis of perceived value of information sources for decision making.

The first utility, the format of an information source, is the package containing the information. If a person is not willing to select information because it appears in a special format, such as a computer print-out, microfiche, or audiovisual, then the format becomes a negative criterion or utility for the individual. Format of an information source takes on increased importance with the increased use of nontraditional or technological formats for presenting information.

The second information utility, form, has to do with the language or jargon in which it is presented, the use of sophisticated mathematical techniques, and its general clarity. The appropriateness of the form of information will be closely related to the style in which the information is presented as well as the level of comprehension that is needed to understand the information. "As the form of information more closely matches the requirements of the decision maker, its value (or utility) increases."[5]

Another utility is timeliness. If an information source is selected to resolve a specific decision situation it must be made available to the decision maker before the decision is reached. This aspect of timeliness should not be confused with that of current information, which may be a component of accuracy. Timely information is a utility because it is not content-related; if the information, regardless of content, does not reach the decision maker in time to provide input for the decision situation, its value is negligible.

The final utility is availability. Selection of an information source is strongly influenced by its ease of access.[6] The less difficulty associated with accessing an information source, the more likely it is that the source will be selected. Availability, for the professional librarian, can be examined both in terms of physical and bibliographic availability. Ultimately, personal possession of an information source is likely to be preferred because of ease, bibliographic availability, and physical availability.

The variables suggested in the model are dimensions of the concept of perceived value of information sources. Empirical evidence suggests that identifiable dimensions of information are related to the perceived value of information.[7] Although the definitions for those dimensions vary somewhat from those employed in this chapter, they provide support for the use of accuracy, cost, benefit, and the utilities of format, form, timeliness, and availability as primary variables to estimate perceived value. These dimensions, in themselves, may be multidimensional; however, for the purposes of this study, perceived value of an information source selected for a specific decision situation will be defined by the above variables or dimensions.

Specifics on the methodology of the information evaluation study are described in Chapter 3. The data collection instrument is presented in Appendix II. Overall, the purpose of the study was to investigate academic librarians' perceived value of various types of information sources as input to the decision-making process. It is recognized that respondents' perceived value is a broad concept that includes the various dimensions previously described. Henceforth the use of the term perceived value is meant to describe this broad concept and is understood to mean the function of the interrelationship among the non-utilities and utilities described above.

Within this concept of perceived value of information sources selected for decision making, findings from this study will be presented. Data were collected on respondents' first, second, and last choice of information sources for specific decision situations; however, the findings will emphasize first choice selections. A summary of first choice selections will be presented followed by an examination of information source preferences by administrative jobtype. The selection of information sources will then be related to various social-organizational characteristics as well as to specific decision situations to identify any significant relationships. Next, an analysis of library decision situations based on information sources selected will be presented. The chapter concludes by suggesting that information sources preferred as input for decision making are similar for all kinds of individuals but are severely limited in diversity. Implications of these and other findings are discussed.

INFORMATION SOURCES SELECTED

As suggested in the introduction to this chapter, the selection of an information source for a specific decision situation is a complex process. In this section a description of *what* information sources are selected will be emphasized rather than *how* or *why* sources are selected. The information sources and decision situations under investigation throughout this chapter are summarized in Table 6-1. Because the various decision situations and information sources are coded by letters and numbers, respectively, it may be necessary to refer to this figure when examining other figures in this chapter.

TABLE 6-1

Information Sources and Decision Situations

I. TYPES OF INFORMATION SOURCES

A. Interpersonal contact (with)
   1. professional staff in library
   2. paraprofessional staff in library
   3. library patrons (users)
   4. librarians outside the library
   5. faculty members
   6. vendors, jobbers, salespersons

B. Written documents
   7. books
   8. articles from library-related periodicals or journals
   9. book reviews
   10. articles from journals not related directly to librarianship
   11. brochures, advertisements, flyers, etc.
   12. reports or statistical information produced by staff members in your library

C. Group or organizational
   13. committee or group meetings composed of library staff
   14. committee or group meetings with non-library staff from the universi
   15. committee or group meetings of professional organizations (ALA, SLA, etc.)
   16. continuing education

D. Personal
   17. past experiences
   18. personal opinion
   19. doing some research on my own t analyze decision situation
   20. other

II. DECISION SITUATIONS

A. Automation of circulation
B. Evaluation of candidates for a new position
C. Purchasing books or other materials for the library
D. How to equitably allocate the acquisitions budget
E. How to reorganize the floor space of the library work areas and stacking areas
F. Whether the library should increase or decrease hours of operation

G. Providing on-line data base reference service
H. Establishing or improving the library security system
I. Implementing copyright procedures for the library
J. Joining a union or collective bargaining unit
K. How to equitably evaluate library personnel
L. Joining a cooperative bibliographic network

The selection of an information source as input for a specific library decision is a perceived estimate of the value of a given source. This perceived value is a combination of a number of dimensions previously described. However, the data collection process in this study is quite similar to a real-world situation. Imagine, for instance, that the librarian has been selected by the director to participate on a committee whose purpose is to investigate the feasibility of implementing a security system for the library. The librarian, somewhat unfamiliar with this topic, asks, "Where can I go to obtain some information about security systems?"

After some consideration, based on a perceived evaluation of a vast array of possible sources, the librarian decides which source to examine first. It is this process that is being replicated during the data collection process. The librarians are asked to indicate from a list of twenty possible sources their first choice for an information source as input to a specific decision situation. Table 6-2 summarizes the selection preferences for the decision situations studied.

The first column of Table 6-2 lists the decision situations posed to participants in the study. The second column, "#1 Rank," presents the number of the information source (see Figure 6-1 for explanation) most often selected as input for the decision situation followed by the percentage of *total* selections that information source explained for that decision situation. The second, third, and fourth most frequently selected sources are presented in the next columns. The last column, "Percent Included as First Four Choices," describes the total percentage of selections encompassed in the top four sources compared to all selections for that decision situation.

The data in Table 6-2 suggest that a few sources tend to account for a vast majority of the selections. The most preferred information source as input for five of the decisions is articles from library-related periodicals or journals (source 8). This heavy reliance on information from the library-related journals and periodicals is somewhat surprising given the informal and formal criticism usually attached to the value of such materials.[8]

A closer examination of the decision situations in which journals are selected as first preference or second preference provides an explanation. For the following decision situations, journals were a first or second preference:

1. automation of circulation
2. providing on-line data base service
3. establishing or improving library security system
4. implementing copyright procedures
5. how to equitably evaluate library personnel
6. joining a bibliographic network

TABLE 6-2

Summary of First Choice Selections
as Input to Specific Decision Situations

DECISION SITUATIONS	#1 RANK Source No.	Percent	#2 RANK Source No.	Percent
A. Automation of circulation	8	41	4	29
B. Evaluation of candidates for a new position	1	35	13	17
C. Purchasing books or other materials for the library	9	47	5	12
D. How to equitably allocate the acquisitions budget	1	21	13	18
E. How to reorganize the floor space of the library work areas and stacking areas	1	28	13	23
F. Whether the library should increase or decrease hours of operation	3	34	12	22
G. Providing on-line data base reference service	8	26	1	17
H. Establishing or improving the library security system	8	29	13	17
I. Implementing copyright procedures for the library	8	37	13	15
J. Joining a union or collective bargaining unit	18	22	1	21
K. How to equitably evaluate library personnel	8	20	1	18
L. Joining a cooperative bibliographic network	4	31	8	26

#3 RANK Source No.	Percent	#4 RANK Source No.	Percent	PERCENT INCLUDED AS FIRST FOUR CHOICES
13	6	1	4	80
18	14	17	11	77
1	10	6	6	75
12	17	8	15	81
8	15	19	11	77
13	17	1	9	82
4	15	16	11	69
1	15	12	14	75
1	11	16	10	73
13	20	4	15	78
13	17	19	15	70
1	11	13	11	79

One characteristic common to all of these decision situations is currency. Each has to do with a current high-interest topic facing the profession. Furthermore, five of the six decision situations relate to technology or technically complex operations. Despite the lengthy time lag for journal publications, the journal literature is preferred for current technologically oriented decision situations.

A second finding indicates the limited preferences for source 12 (reports or statistical information produced by staff members in your library) or source 19 (doing some research on my own to analyze the decision situation). Neither of these two sources is preferred for any decision situation. They are selected only once as second most often preferred, once as third most often preferred, and twice as fourth most often preferred. These findings suggest that professional librarians rely on generalized sources of information. They conduct little research on decision situations, which results in few internal studies available for consultation. Furthermore, this finding suggests that information input used from generalized noninstitutional sources is likely not to consider environmental or institutional factors unique to the library facing a specific decision situation.

A summary of the information source preferences for all decision situations is presented in Figure 6-1. In this graph each information source is ranked in order of the percentage of times it was selected for *all* decision situations compared to selections made. Overall, the most frequently selected information source is 8, articles from library-related periodicals or journals; the second most frequently selected information source is 1, interpersonal contact with professional librarians in the library; and the third is 13, committee or group meetings. Together, these sources account for almost 50 percent of all selections.

Another interesting feature of Figure 6-1 is the nature of the curve itself. Clearly, the curve is hyperbolic and can be described as a modified Yule distribution. This type of curve has been identified often in bibliometric studies in information science. In generalized terms, the curve simply says that a large portion of "items" or, in this case, a large portion of the selections involves a relatively few sources.

In such situations one is reminded of Trueswell's 80-20 rule which suggests that 80 percent of library circulation requirements are satisfied by approximately 20 percent of the library's holdings.[9] Similar relationships also have been found regarding journal use and journal citations. In these

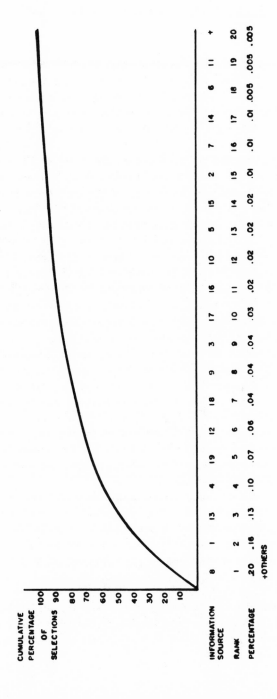

FIGURE 6-1 Summary of Information Source Preferences for All Decision Situations

situations, Yule distributions are found consistently.[10] One wonders if the distribution holds true for the selection of information source.

A closer examination of the curve depicted in Figure 6-1 does not support an 80-20 rule for the selection of all information sources. In this case, 80 percent of the selection requirements are satisfied by 40 percent of the sources. However, it must be kept in mind that Figure 6-1 is a summary of *all* information source selections for *all* decision situations.

Referring to Figure 6-2, an entirely different conclusion can be reached. Because there were twenty possible sources to be selected by an individual, the first four sources represent 20 percent of all possible sources. The last column in Figure 6-2 indicates the cumulative percentage of all available selections that the first four sources represent *for each decision situation.* In this analysis it is striking that the cumulative percentage varies around 80 percent. In short, Trueswell's 80-20 rule appears to hold true for selection of information sources for a specific decision situation: approximately 80 percent of the selection requirements are satisfied by 20 percent of the information sources.

INFORMATION SELECTION AND
ADMINISTRATIVE JOBTYPE

Participants in this study were categorized according to their administrative responsibilities. The following categories were defined:

1. *Top Administration.* This term included the director and any assistant or associate directors.
2. *Department Head.* A librarian who supervises at least one other professional.
3. *Area or Section Head.* A librarian who supervises paraprofessionals but no other professionals.
4. *Nonadministration.* A librarian who does not supervise other library employees.

Based on these categories and definitions it is possible to describe the selection of information sources based on administrative responsibility.

	SEX	AGE	ADMINISTRATIVE RESPONSIBILITY	EDUCATION	LIBRARY EXPERIENCE	PROFESSIONAL EXPERIENCE
SEX						
AGE	-					
ADMINISTRATIVE RESPONSIBILITY	-	.01				
EDUCATION	.05	-	.02			
LIBRARY EXPERIENCE	-	.001	.001	-		
PROFESSIONAL EXPERIENCE	-	.001	.001	-	.001	
EFFECT OF INFORMATIONAL INPUT ON DECISION MAKING	.05	-	.001	.02	.01	.01

Explanation: Table represents levels of significance between the two variables.

FIGURE 6-2   Relationship between Social-Organizational Variables

A summary of group characteristics is presented for top administration, department heads, area heads, and nonadministrative librarians in Table 6-3. No surprises appear in this table. Five variables are positively related to each other: age, education, years of library experience, total years of professional experience, and effect of information input on decision making. As one increases, the others tend to increase as well. The higher the individual's formal status in the organization, the greater the number of years of library and professional experience and level of formal education of the individual are likely to be.

Table 6-4 summarizes the information source selections by administrative jobtype. For each administrative category the most often selected and second most often selected first choice information sources are presented. With each source also is the percentage of selections that the source represents for that particular decision situation. For instance, the most frequently selected information source by top administration as input for decision situation A, automation of circulation, is source 4, interpersonal contact with librarians outside the library. This source was selected 33 percent of the time by top administration in this particular decision situation.

An inspection of this table suggests that, overall, there is little difference among administrative jobtypes in perceived value of information sources for specific decision situations. Automation of circulation, allocating the acquisitions budget, reorganizing floor space, hours of operation, on-line reference service, security system, copyright, and joining a cooperative bibliographic network each have similar source selections by all four groups. The other decision situations have less agreement but, overall, are still remarkably similar.

A number of additional observations can be made from this table. First, sources 2 (contact with paraprofessionals), 6 (vendors, jobbers, and salespersons), 7 (books), 10 (articles from nonlibrary-related journals), 11 (brochures, flyers, etc.), 14 (committee meetings with nonlibrary staff from the university), and 16 (continuing education workshops) are not listed as most frequently or second most frequently selected as input to a decision situation by any of the administrative groups. The overall perceived value of these sources as input to a decision situation suggests that accuracy, cost, benefits, and other utilities of these sources are seen to be of limited value.

A second observation is that top administration selected nine first-choice selections that were categorized as interpersonal, department heads selected six, area heads selected two, and nonadministration heads selected

TABLE 6-3

Group Characteristics of Top Administration, Department Heads, Area Heads, and Nonadministrative Librarians

ADMINISTRA-TIVE TYPE	GROUP CHARACTERISTIC									
	Sex (%)		Age	Education				Years Experience in Present Library	Total Years Experience	Effect of Informational Input on Decision Making**
	M	F		B.A.	M.L.S.	M.L.S.+*	Ph.D.			
Top Administration (N=12)	58	42	48	8	34	33	25	14	19	6.0
Department Head (N=15)	27	73	45	7	60	13	20	9	17	4.6
Area Head*** (N=26)	30	65	37	0	73	21	0	8	11	3.3
Nonadministration (N=13)	23	77	37	0	69	31	0	3	7	2.8

*M.L.S.+ = M.L.S. plus subject master's.
**Effect of informational input on decision making is scaled from 1 = no effect to 7 = very great effect.
***One Area Head did not respond to the questions regarding sex and education, therefore the percentages do not equal 100%.

TABLE 6-4

Information Source Selections
by Administrative Jobtype

DECISION SITUATIONS	Top (N=12)				Dept. (N=15)			
	1st Choice		2nd Choice		1st Choice		2nd Choice	
	Source*	Percent	Source*	Percent	Source*	Percent	Source*	Percent
A. Automation of circulation	4	33	8	25	4	46	8	33
B. Evaluation of candidates for a new position	1	58	13	15	18	20	13	13
C. Purchasing books or other materials for the library	1	33	5	25	9	40	5	20
D. How to equitably allocate the acquisitions budget	1	33	12	25	1	20	12	20
E. How to reorganize the floor space of the library work areas and stacking areas	1	58	13	16	13	26	1	20
F. Whether the library should increase or decrease hours of operation	3	33	12	33	3	26	13	20
G. Providing on-line data base reference service	1	33	8	33	4	26	8	20
H. Establishing or improving the library security system	8	33	1	16	8	40	12	33
I. Implementing copyright procedures for the library	8	33	13	16	8	53	19	13
J. Joining a union or collective bargaining unit	4	25	1	16	1	33	13	27
K. How to equitably evaluate library personnel	13	33	1	16	1	33	8	27
L. Joining a cooperative bibliographic network	4	42	8	25	8	33	4	27

*See Table 6-1 for description of information source codes.

JOBTYPE

| | Area (N=26) | | | | Nonadmin. (N=13) | | |
| 1st Choice | | 2nd Choice | | 1st Choice | | 2nd Choice | |
Source*	Percent	Source*	Percent	Source*	Percent	Source*	Percent
8	38	4	27	8	61	4	07
1	42	13	15	13	23	17	20
9	42	5	07	9	92	18	07
13	30	1	19	1	14	13	07
13	23	8	15	1	39	13	23
3	30	13	26	3	46	12	30
8	27	1	23	8	23	4	23
8	23	13	19	8	30	1	23
8	27	13	19	8	30	13	15
18	23	1	19	18	46	4	23
8	23	1	19	13	30	18	23
8	27	4	23	4	39	15	23

four. Such a ranking may suggest that the greater one's formal authority in the organization, the greater the perceived value of interpersonal sources.

A third observation from Table 6-3 is the limited perceived value of information source 12 (reports or statistical information produced by staff) and source 19 (doing some research on my own). The data reinforce similar findings from Table 6-2. However, the data from Table 6-4 suggest that the limited perceived value of these sources is held by all four administrative jobtypes. Reasons for such perception might include limited time to conduct research or produce reports, personnel who are not skilled in research or statistical techniques, or simply that expected benefits from such sources are seen as limited. Regardless of the specific reasons for such a perception, original "hard data" are perceived to be of little value as input to these decision situations.

As suggested in Table 6-1, the information sources were categorized as interpersonal, written, group or organizational, and personal. Based on these categories a chi-square goodness-of-fit test was performed between those categories and the administrative jobtype categories for each decision situation. Data from all four libraries were analyzed to determine if the categories of information sources selected by each administrative jobtype were similar for the various decision situations. A 2 X 4 contingency table was produced to relate the four information source categories to two administrative jobtypes, such as top administration and all others. Tables were produced for each jobtype in this fashion. A summary of significant relationships is presented in Table 6-5. Those relationships in which the hypothesis "categories of information sources selected by one jobtype are similar to those selected by all other jobtypes" is accepted are indicated by a "—." Where the hypothesis has been rejected, a level of significance is indicated.

Overall, categories of information sources selected by all administrative jobtypes are remarkably similar for the various decision situations. Only in five instances does one jobtype select information source categories that are significantly different from the categories selected by all other participants for that particular decision situation. These instances are explained as follows:

1. *Evaluation of candidates for a new position.* Department heads perceive written sources to be most valuable, whereas others prefer interpersonal sources.

TABLE 6-5

Relationship between Administrative Jobtype
and Categories of Information Sources
Selected for Specific Decision Situations

DECISION SITUATIONS	ADMINISTRATIVE JOBTYPE			
	Top	Dept.	Area	Nonadmin.
A. Automation of circulation	—	—	—	—
B. Evaluation of candidates for a new position	—	.001	—	—
C. Purchasing books or other materials for the library	.005	—	—	.02
D. How to equitably allocate the acquisitions budget	.05	—	—	—
E. How to reorganize the floor space of the library work areas and stacking areas	—	—	—	—
F. Whether the library should increase or decrease hours of operation	—	.07	—	—
G. Providing on-line data base reference service	—	—	—	—
H. Establishing or improving the library security system	—	—	—	—
I. Implementing copyright procedures for the library	—	—	—	—
J. Joining a union or collective bargaining unit	—	—	—	—
K. How to equitably evaluate library personnel	—	—	—	—
L. Joining a cooperative bibliographic network	—	—	—	—

2. *Purchasing books or other materials.* Top administration perceived interpersonal sources to be most valuable whereas others prefer written sources; nonadministrative employees perceive written sources as most valuable, but top administrators prefer interpersonal sources.

3. *Equitable allocation of the acquisitions budget.* Top administration perceives little value in group/organizational sources whereas others prefer group/organizational sources.

4. *Increase or decrease hours of operation.* Department heads perceive no category to be especially valuable whereas others prefer interpersonal sources.

Generally, in those cases where a significant difference in perceived value of information sources exists, department heads tend to perceive written sources as more valuable whereas others, especially top administrators, perceive interpersonal sources to be of more value.

Data from Table 6-5 support findings drawn from Table 6-4 that in all administrative jobtypes librarians have similar perceptions of the value of information for specific decision situations. One implication of this lack of diversity of information sources as input for decision situations is a tendency toward a narrow analysis of the situation. Limited source diversity and use of internally generated information sources encourage this narrow view and further suggest the need for expediency in information input for these decision situations.

INFORMATION SELECTION AND SOCIAL-ORGANIZATIONAL VARIABLES

Data from the information evaluation study also were collected on the subject's sex, age, administrative responsibility, education, years of experience in present library, years of professional experience, and perceived effect of informational input on decision making. To facilitate appropriate statistical tests, data from all four libraries were analyzed together, based on the assumption that organizational variables such as structure, size, and potential access to and knowledge of various information sources are similar.

To test the possibility of significant relationships between the social-organizational variables or between social-organizational variables and the selection of information sources, the data were collapsed into categories. Age was categorized as 20 to 35, 36 to 50, and 51 to 65; administrative responsibility was categorized as top administration, department head, area head, and nonadministration; education as B.A., M.L.S., M.L.S.+ (M.L.S. and subject masters), and Ph.D.; and library experience and professional experience as 1 to 10 years, 11 to 20 years, and 20 or more years. Perceived effect of informational input on decision making originally was a scaled response ranging from 1 (no effect) to 7 (very great effect). However, for purposes of analysis those responding with a 1, 2, or 3 were grouped together as "little effect," and those responding with a 5, 6, or 7 were grouped together as "great effect." Throughout the remainder of this chapter, a chi-square test of association between the variables was used to identify relationships. Only where the level of significance was .05 or less are the scores reported.

Figure 6-2 presents a summary of significant relationships between the various social-organizational variables. A closer inspection of the specific contingency tables producing these levels of significance helps to explain why the relationships were found to be significant. The relationship between sex and education was significant because males tend to have more formal education than women. A significant relationship also was identified between sex and perceived effect of information input on decision making; females tend to categorize themselves as having little effect, whereas males tend to categorize themselves as having great effect on decision making.

Age appears to be significantly related to administrative responsibility, years of present library experience, and years of professional experience. Not surprisingly, the older a librarian is, the greater the likelihood of his or her having increased administrative responsibility and more years of library and professional experience. Administrative responsibility is also significantly related to education, library experience, professional experience, and perceived effect of informational input on decision making.

Perhaps most striking are the significant relationships between perceived effect of information input on decision making and five of the six social-organizational variables. The data suggest that those men with greater administrative responsibility and more formal education and substantial library and professional experience tend to have greater effect on decision making than others in the organization. These findings support the obvious situations in many academic libraries. They suggest that female librarians, for a host of reasons, have limited effect on library decision making. Furthermore, these findings support similar findings in Chapters 4 and 5 of the information contact study.

Data from the information evaluation study also can be analyzed to better understand the relationship between the selection of information sources and social-organizational characteristics. Are a person's social-organizational characteristics related to the selection of certain types of information for specific decision situations? To address this question, information sources were analyzed in terms of each of the following possible categories:

1. internal/external
2. oral/written
3. interpersonal/written/group/personal

Table 6-6 summarizes the information sources defined as internal/external and oral/written. In general, a source was considered to be internal if it originated within the organization. Oral sources are those of a verbal or personal nature. A summary of the specific information sources defined as interpersonal, written, group, or personal appears in Table 6-1.

The purpose of using three different techniques to categorize the information sources is to examine the proposition that socio-organizational variables are not related to the selection of information sources regardless of the method by which they are categorized. Furthermore, the information sources had to be categorized into groups in order that contingency tables relating the variables would have enough cases per cell for a chi-square test to be performed. To make the data more meaningful, the relationships between social-organizational variables and the selection of information sources were determined within the context of a specific decision situation.

Table 6-7 summarizes the relationship between the selection of internal/external sources and social-organizational variables for the various decision situations. For those relationships in which the data do not

TABLE 6-6

Summary of Internal/External and
Oral/Written Categories of Information Sources

INTERNAL/EXTERNAL INFORMATION SOURCES

Internal

1. Professional staff in library
2. Paraprofessional staff in library
3. Library patrons (users)
12. Reports or statistical information produced by library staff members
13. Committee or group meetings of library staff members
17. Past experiences
18. Personal opinions
19. Doing some research on my own

External

4. Librarians outside the library
5. Faculty members
6. Vendors, jobbers, salespersons
7. Books
8. Articles from library-related journals
9. Book reviews
10. Articles from journals not directly related to librarianship
11. Brochures, advertisements, flyers
14. Committee or group meetings with nonlibrary staff members
15. Committee or group meetings of professional organizations
16. Continuing education workshops

ORAL/WRITTEN INFORMATION SOURCES

Oral

1. Professional staff in library
2. Paraprofessional staff in library
3. Library patrons
4. Librarians outside library
5. Faculty members
6. Vendors, jobbers, salespersons
13. Committee or group meetings of library staff members
14. Committee or group meetings with nonlibrary staff members
15. Committee or group meetings of professional organizations
16. Continuing education workshops
17. Past experiences
18. Personal opinions

Written

7. Books
8. Articles from library-related periodicals or journals
9. Book reviews
10. Articles from journals not directly related to librarianship
11. Brochures, advertisements, flyers
12. Reports or statistical information produced by staff members
19. Doing some research on my own

TABLE 6-7

Relationship between the Selection of
Internal/External Sources and Social-
Organizational Variables

DECISION SITUATIONS	Sex	Age
A. Automation of circulation	.02[a]	—
B. Evaluation of candidates for a new position	—	—
C. Purchasing books or other materials for the library	.04[b]	.03[c]
D. How to equitably allocate the acquisitions budget	—	—
E. How to reorganize the floor space of the library work areas and stacking areas	—	.02[d]
F. Whether the library should increase or decrease hours of operation	—	—
G. Providing on-line data base reference service	—	—
H. Establishing or improving the library security system	—	—
I. Implementing copyright procedures for the library	—	—
J. Joining a union or collective bargaining unit	—	—
K. How to equitably evaluate library personnel	—	—
L. Joining a cooperative bibliographic network	—	—

[a]Females tend to prefer external sources; men have no preference.
[b]Females tend to prefer external sources; men have no perference.
[c]Age 20 to 35 and 50 to 65 prefer external; 35 to 50 have no preference.
[d]Age 20 to 35 and 35 to 50 prefer internal; 50 to 65 have no preference.
[e]M.L.S. and M.L.S.+ prefer external; B.A. and Ph.D. prefer internal sources.
[f]Those having great effect prefer internal; others prefer external.

Administrative Responsibility	Education	Library Experience	Professional Experience	Effect of Informational Input on Decision Making
—	—	—	—	—
—	—	—	—	—
—	.01[e]	—	—	—
—	—	—	—	—
—	—	—	—	—
—	—	—	—	—
—	—	—	—	.02[f]
—	—	—	—	—
—	—	—	—	—
—	—	—	—	—
—	—	—	—	—
—	—	—	—	—

follow an expected distribution and are significant at the .05 level or less, the actual significance level is indicated. All other relationships were found to follow the expected distributions. Overall, very few relationships (six out of eighty-four) have significance levels of .05 or less. For those instances in which a significant relationship was identified, an explanation is provided.

A closer examination of the specific decision situations where at least one social-organizational variable appears to be significantly related is interesting. Females tend to prefer external sources regarding automation of circulation, perhaps because they are not part of the "Old Boy" structure in the library. The same may hold true for their preferences regarding the purchase of material. It is notable that three social-organizational variables appear to be related to the selection of internal or external sources regarding the purchase of material: sex, age, and education.

A second method to categorize the information sources is oral/written. Table 6-8 summarizes the relationship between the selection of oral/written sources and social-organizational variables for each of the various decision situations. Only in those situations when the relationship is significant are the levels of significance presented. Similar to the preceding figure, there are few instances (eight out of eighty-four) in which significant relationships are identified. In such instances, an explanation is provided at the bottom of the figure.

For the decision "purchasing books or other materials for the library" age, administrative responsibility, library experience, professional experience, and effect of informational input on decision making are significant factors. Some common relationships between variables are (1) younger librarians with limited experience prefer written sources, and (2) librarians with great effect on decision making or who are top administrators prefer oral sources. But the significant preferences within the social-organizational variables are limited to two decisions: purchase of books and material for the library and allocation of the acquisitions budget.

The data in Table 6-9 suggest that for some decision situations the category of preferred information sources is quite different from other decision situations. Based on this method of categorization the relationship between categories of sources and social-organizational variables can be examined. Table 6-10 summarizes those instances when significant relationships were identified for a specific decision situation. Again, very few of the relationships (eight out of eighty-four) were found to be significant.

The data in Table 6-10 support the previous two tables on the relationship between selection of information sources and social-organizational variables. Especially interesting is that once again, decision situation C (purchase of books or other material) has five variables significantly related to selection of information sources. Overall, the findings suggest that (1) younger librarians with limited experience prefer written sources to interpersonal sources, and (2) top administrators or those librarians with great effect on decision making prefer interpersonal sources. But, for the vast majority of decisions, the social-organizational variables do not appear to be related to the selection of information sources.

In those instances when there is a significant relationship between the selection of information sources (regardless of how categorized) and social-organizational variables, the following explanations may be likely. Those librarians who find themselves outside the decision-making clique (as suggested in Chapter 5), such as younger librarians, librarians with less experience, and female librarians, tend to prefer written external sources. Their "preference" may be due less to a conscious effort on their part to select such material than to the simple fact that they do not have access to those sources of information from people inside the library.

Despite this consideration, the notion that preferences for information sources are not related to social-organizational variables appears to be supported except for one decision situation, purchase of books or other material for the library. As a group, academic librarians in this study perceive similar information sources to be of value for specific decision situations. This finding is supported regardless of the librarian's social-organizational characteristics and regardless of how the information sources are categorized.

DESCRIBING DECISIONS BASED ON INFORMATION SOURCES

The complexity of describing the decision-making process has been discussed in Chapter 2. However, it may be possible to describe a decision situation based on the perceived value of information sources selected as

TABLE 6-8

Relationship between the Selection of
Oral/Written Sources and Social-
Organizational Variables

DECISION SITUATIONS	Sex	Age
A. Automation of circulation	—	—
B. Evaluation of candidates for a new position	—	—
C. Purchasing books or other materials for the library	—	.001[a]
D. How to equitably allocate the acquisitions budget	—	.01[b]
E. How to reorganize the floor space of the library work areas and stacking areas	—	—
F. Whether the library should increase or decrease hours of operation	—	—
G. Providing on-line data base reference service	—	—
H. Establishing or improving the library security system	—	—
I. Implementing copyright procedures for the library	—	—
J. Joining a union or collective bargaining unit	—	—
K. How to equitably evaluate library personnel	—	—
L. Joining a cooperative bibliographic network	—	—

[a]The 20 to 35 age group prefers written; all others prefer oral sources.
[b]The 20 to 35 age group prefers written; all others prefer oral sources.
[c]All administrative types have overwhelming preference for oral sources.
[d]Top administration and department heads prefer oral sources; area heads and nonadministration prefer written sources.
[e]Those with 0 to 10 years prefer written; those with 10 to 20 years prefer oral sources.
[f]The greater the years of professional experience, the greater the preference for oral sources.
[g]Those with 10 to 20 and more than 20 years experience prefer oral sources; those with 0 to 10 years professional experience prefer written sources.
[h]Those with great effect prefer oral sources; those with little effect prefer written sources.

Administrative Responsibility	Education	Library Experience	Professional Experience	Effect of Informational Input on Decision Making
—	—	—	—	—
.01[c]	—	—	—	—
.01[d]	—	.01[e]	.01[f]	.01[h]
—	—	—	.03[g]	—
—	—	—	—	—
—	—	—	—	—
—	—	—	—	—
—	—	—	—	—
—	—	—	—	—
—	—	—	—	—
—	—	—	—	—
—	—	—	—	—

TABLE 6-9

Percentage of Sources Categorized as
Interpersonal, Written, Group, or Personal
Selected for Each Decision Situation

DECISION SITUATIONS	INTERPERSONAL	WRITTEN	GROUP	PERSONAL
A. Automation of circulation	38	47	9	6
B. Evaluation of candidates for a new position	45	5	16	34
C. Purchasing books or other materials for the library	35	57	2	6
D. How to equitably allocate the acquisitions budget	26	34	22	18
E. How to reorganize the floor space of the library work areas and stacking areas	34	25	25	16
F. Whether the library should increase or decrease hours of operation	49	22	19	10
G. Providing on-line data base reference service	41	29	24	6
H. Establishing or improving the library security system	28	47	19	6
I. Implementing copyright procedures for the library	17	46	31	6
J. Joining a union or collective bargaining unit	33	20	19	28
K. How to equitably evaluate library personnel	22	34	20	24
L. Joining a cooperative bibliographic network	41	29	20	10

input for that decision situation. Such a procedure assumes that there are dimensions of information sources that may be used as criteria to analyze a specific decision situation. Furthermore, if the dimensions are considered to be continuums, each decision situation can be plotted along these continuums based on some score resulting from the selection of information sources for that particular decision situation.

In the strictest sense of the word, a continuum is a set in which no distinction of content can be made except by reference to some other characteristic. Typically, the continuum represents an uninterrupted ordinal sequence of possible scores between the characteristic (measure) and the concept being considered. True continuums in social science inquiry are unusual. One approach to examine a concept on a continuum basis is to identify two opposite points on the scale and assume a continuous measure between the two.

This procedure will be employed for describing each decision situation in terms of the information sources perceived to be most valuable as input. For purposes of this analysis two dimensions are suggested: origin of the information source and channel of the information source. The two opposites for origin are internal (originated within the library) and external (originated outside the library). The two opposites for channel are oral (information obtained orally or personally) and written (information that is carried by a secondary form—such as memos, books, articles). These two dimensions will be treated as continuums. Thus, a two-dimensional graph can be produced to plot the relative score of each decision in relation to each dimension.

Specific information sources have been identified as either oral or written and internal or external and are described in Table 6-6. Based on these criteria, it is possible to determine the percentage of sources categorized as either internal/external or oral/written for each decision situation. These percentages are presented in Table 6-11. In reading this table, it can be seen, for instance, that 15 percent of the information sources selected as input for the decision situation "automation of circulation" are categorized as internal sources and eighty-five percent as external. For the same decision situation, the breakdown between preferences for oral and written sources is 52 percent preferred oral sources and forty-eight percent preferred written.

An examination of sources selected when categorized as either oral/written or internal/external presents some revealing findings. First, in

TABLE 6-10

Relationship between the Selection of
Interpersonal/Written/Group/Personal
Sources and Social-Organizational Variables

DECISION SITUATIONS	Sex	Age
A. Automation of circulation	—	—
B. Evaluation of candidates for a new position	—	—
C. Purchasing books or other materials for the library	—	.004[b]
D. How to equitably allocate the acquisitions budget	—	.03[c]
E. How to reorganize the floor space of the library work areas and stacking areas	—	—
F. Whether the library should increase or decrease hours of operation	.03[a]	—
G. Providing on-line data base reference service	—	—
H. Establishing or improving the library security system	—	—
I. Implementing copyright procedures for the library	—	—
J. Joining a union or collective bargaining unit	—	—
K. How to equitably evaluate library personnel	—	—
L. Joining a cooperative bibliographic network	—	—

[a] Females prefer interpersonal sources; males have no preference.
[b] Age 20 to 35 prefer written; other age groups prefer interpersonal sources.
[c] Age 20 to 35 prefer written; other age groups prefer interpersonal sources.
[d] Top administration prefers interpersonal sources; others have no preference.
[e] Top administration prefers interpersonal sources; others have no preference.
[f] Those with 0 to 10 years experience prefer written; others prefer interpersonal.
[g] Those with 0 to 10 years experience prefer written; others prefer interpersonal.
[h] Those with great effect prefer interpersonal sources; those with little effect prefer written sources.

SOCIAL-ORGANIZATIONAL VARIABLES				
Administrative Responsibility	Education	Library Experience	Professional Experience	Effect of Informational Input on Decision Making
—	—	—	—	—
.007[d]	—	—	—	—
.01[e]	—	.006[f]	.01[g]	.02[h]
—	—	—	—	—
—	—	—	—	—
—	—	—	—	—
—	—	—	—	—
—	—	—	—	—
—	—	—	—	—
—	—	—	—	—
—	—	—	—	—
—	—	—	—	—

all but one decision situation is the general preference for an oral source rather than a written source. Only in the case of decision situation C (purchase of books or other materials for the library) is the overall preference for a written source. This finding is especially interesting, because the single most preferred source (regardless of decision situation) is source 8 (articles from library-related journals). Yet when the source selections are categorized overall as oral/written, more total preferences for oral sources are apparent for specific decision situations.

A second point for consideration is the general preference for external information sources as input for specific decision situations. In only three of the twelve decision situations is there overall preference for internal information sources: evaluation of candidates, allocation of the acquisitions budget, and whether the library should increase or decrease hours of operation. This finding contrasts with the overall finding that the second and third most preferred individual sources (regardless of decision situations) are 1 (interpersonal contact with other librarians in the library) and 13 (committee or group meeting of librarians in the library). Apparently, actual preferences *for specific decision situations* is more realistically represented by Table 6-11.

Based on source preferences categorized as oral/written and internal/external, it is possible to plot the decisions on a two-dimensional graph. Such a graph would have a continuum representing the sources selected for a specific decision, divided into oral/written and internal/external sources. The score for each decision situation is determined by the following method. For decision situation A, automation of circulation, thirty-four respondents preferred oral sources and thirty-one preferred written sources. Overall there is a preference for oral sources by a count of three. If the X axis on a graph represents oral/written sources then the X score is three toward the end representing oral sources. The same procedure is used for the Y axis, which will represent internal/external source preferences for the various decision situations. In this example for automation of circulation, ten respondents preferred internal sources and fifty-five preferred external sources, thus, indicating an overall preference for external sources of forty-five. Therefore, the Y score is forty-five toward that end representing external sources. With both X and Y axis scores for the information source preferences, a graph can be constructed such as that depicted in Figure 6-3.

TABLE 6-11

Percentage of Sources Categorized as
Internal/External or Oral/Written
Selected for Each Decision Situation

DECISION SITUATIONS	INTERNAL	EXTERNAL	ORAL	WRITTEN
A. Automation of circulation	15	85	52	48
B. Evaluation of candidates for a new position	67	33	95	5
C. Purchasing books or other materials for the library	20	80	41	59
D. How to equitably allocate the acquisitions budget	57	43	66	34
E. How to reorganize the floor space of the library working areas and stacking areas	50	50	73	27
F. Whether the library should increase or decrease hours of operation	78	22	78	22
G. Providing on-line data base reference services	30	70	70	30
H. Establishing or improving the library security system	38	62	52	48
I. Implementing copyright procedures for the library	17	83	53	47
J. Joining a union or collective bargaining unit	47	53	80	20
K. How to equitably evaluate library personnel	46	54	65	35
L. Joining a cooperative bibliographic network	23	77	70	30

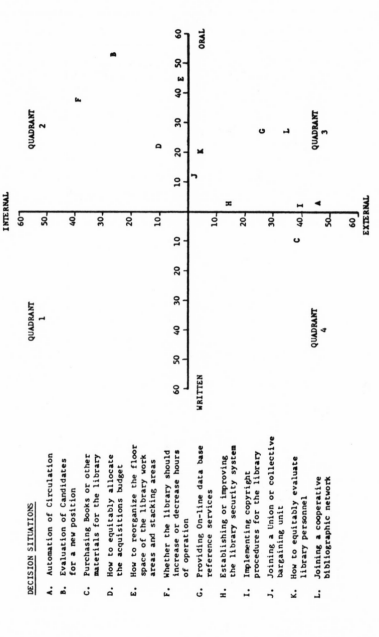

FIGURE 6-3 Decision Situations Described by Selection of Internal/External and Written/Oral Information Sources

DECISION SITUATIONS

A. Automation of Circulation

B. Evaluation of Candidates for a new position

C. Purchasing Books or other materials for the library

D. How to equitably allocate the acquisitions budget

E. How to reorganize the floor space of the library work areas and stacking areas

F. Whether the library should increase or decrease hours of operation

G. Providing On-line data base reference services

H. Establishing or improving the library security system

I. Implementing copyright procedures for the library

J. Joining a Union or collective bargaining unit

K. How to equitably evaluate library personnel

L. Joining a cooperative bibliographic network

This method of analysis has some limitations, one of which is that, statistically, there is a greater number of possible source combinations that fall into quadrants 2 and 3 than in 1 and 4. For instance, two sources (reports or statistical information produced by staff members and doing some research on my own) are the only possible sources that can be described as written-internal. However, if one assumes that source preferences are not independent selections but based on perceived value (as discussed in the introduction to this chapter) of information sources, the graph takes on considerable importance.

The visual representation of decision situations categorized according to overall oral/written or internal/external source preferences is striking. If the graph is broken into four quadrants, information source preferences for the various decision situations can be described as follows:

1. Written-Internal—0 decision situations
2. Oral-Internal—4 decision situations
3. Oral-External—7 decision situations
4. Written-External—1 decision situation

Clearly, the information sources perceived as valuable input for most decision situations cannot be described as written-internal or written-external.

An implication of this graph is that in these academic libraries there are few information sources available that are statistical reports or memos or personal research. The perceived value of such sources is limited, not because the source is perceived as valueless but perhaps because very few such sources exist in the typical academic library. If a source is not available it will not be selected, and thus, it certainly will not be perceived as valuable. Such is the case, it appears, for these two sources (reports or statistical information produced by staff members and doing some research on my own).

Another implication of the graph is the seemingly apparent relationship between these dimensions. The greater the preference for selecting an oral source, the more likely it is that the source will also be internal. Or, conversely, the less the preference for an oral source, the more likely the source will also be external. A Pearson product moment correlation of .74, which is significant at the .01 level, confirms the relationship between origin of information source (internal/external) and channel (oral/written). When the correlation is squared, there is a direct estimate of the amount of variance shared by the variables. Thus, r2 equals .54, which suggests that 54 percent of the variance is explained by the relationship between these two variables. Such a relationship appears to be most logical, since the most accessible oral sources are likely to be within the library.

The types of decision situations at the bottom left and top right, the two extremes of the graph, are quite different. Decisions I, A, H, G, and L are all rather complex and most deal with the utilization of technology— automation of circulation, on-line data base services, bibliographic network, and security system. At the other extreme are decisions E, F, B, and D. These decisions have to do with space allocation, hours of operation, candidate evaluation, and allocation of the acquisitions budget. None of these decisions deal with the application of technology. Rather, they are somewhat common library decisions encountered rather frequently in the administration of the library.

Information sources that are oral and internal are easily accessible and require little search effort on the part of the participant. However, as the sources one selects tend to be external, they also tend to be less totally oral and more balanced between oral and written. In other words, such sources are more inaccessible and difficult to search. One might assume that the effort associated with searching and attaining information sources is directly related to perceived difficulty of the decision situation. Thus, the data suggest that the greater the reliance on external-written sources is, the greater the perceived importance of difficulty associated with that decision.

The description of decision situations based on perceived value of information sources provides a fresh means to analyze decision situations in an organizational structure such as the academic library. The significant relationship between origin of information sources and channel of information sources for these decision situations suggests that such a relationship deserves additional research attention. Reliance on the "path of least resistance" in selection of an information source appears to be tempered by the difficulty or importance of the decision for which the information is selected. But those sources that would take the most effort to utilize, such as internal statistical reports and doing some research on my own, are virtually ignored as input to the decision situations examined.

SELECTION, EVALUATION,
AND PERCEIVED VALUE

Throughout this chapter the selection of information sources has been based on *perceived* value. In this sense, the data answer the question, "What information source do you think you would select as input to this decision situation?" As such, the data represent espoused behavior rather than actual behavior. Although one would like to believe that espoused behavior will be the same as actual behavior, this may not be true for some of the respondents.

However, the data are especially useful because they mirror the process of cognition during the selection of an information source. First, there is a perceived need; second, there is a preliminary decision as to which information source will have the greatest "value" vis-à-vis this particular situation. The person's perceived value may rest on a combination of any of the utility or non-utility criteria suggested earlier in this chapter. For a given individual, accuracy of this source may have less value than timeliness or some other criterion. Nonetheless, perceived value of an information source is likely to be the first point at which a decision is made as to the likely usefulness of an information source for a particular decision situation.

After this initial process of selection, an individual actually tries to obtain the selected information source. At this point, the feedback and evaluation process begins to refine the initial selection. An ongoing comparison between the information source selected and the inner value system begins. The discrepancy between perceived and actual is evaluated by the utility and non-utility characteristics of information value. At some point the evaluation/feedback process terminates on a source or number of sources that satisfy both the initial information need and the perceived value structure of the individual. But the feedback loop provides a learning situation for the individual that will be reflected in his or her next selection of an information source. Thus, the perceived value may be an accumulation of past experiences, current perceptions, and the various utility and non-utility information values of the individual.

The assumption that learning takes place because of feedback and evaluation during the selection of information sources is a crucial one. Little research has been done on this issue. However, the learning process is not specifically being investigated in this study. Although logic tells us that learning is likely to take place, obviously, such learning is dependent on an effective evaluation/feedback cycle. If an individual never critically evaluates the effectiveness of the information available in a decision situation, then it is equally likely that no learning about the perceived value of the information source will take place. Given this complex selection process, which is still largely unknown, a most significant finding in this study is the general agreement among respondents on the perceived value of an information source for a given decision situation. As Table 6-2 shows, 80 percent of all information selections are satisfied by only 20 percent of the possible sources. One possible implication of this finding is that through previous learning (the feedback and evaluation of previous selections), librarians in this study have identified a small pool of possible sources that are perceived as valuable as input for a broad range of decision situations.

This finding is supported by a number of analyses. Table 6-5 suggests no significant difference, overall, among the sources selected by the four jobtypes: top administrators, department heads, area heads, and non-administrators. Tables 6-7, 6-8, and 6-10 suggest no significant difference, overall, among the sources selected by librarians based on their sex, age, administrative responsibility, education, library experience, professional experience, or the effect of their information input on decision making. Tables 6-9 and 6-11 suggest no significant differences, overall, among the selection of information sources categorized as (1) internal/external, (2) oral/written, or (3) interpersonal, written, group, or personal.

However, when the information sources selected for specific decisions are described by origin and channel (see Figure 6-3) a significant relationship is identified—not between characteristics of the individual and sources selected but between types of decisions and sources selected. For participants in this study an implicit evaluation of the nature of the decision situation in terms of its perceived difficulty/importance appears to have affected the selection of an oral over a written source and an internal over an external source. This finding supports our earlier model of utility and non-utility characteristics if the difficulty/importance of the decision is considered to be a utility.

Furthermore, Figure 6-3 suggests a pattern by which the relative difficulty/importance of a decision situation can be based on the preferred sources of information for that decision situation. The following additional speculation is based on this graph. The information sources that are most available, timely, and involve the least effort to contact are those in quadrant 2 (oral-internal). Somewhat less accessible are those in quadrant 3 (oral-external), because they consume more search time and effort than other sources. Still more inaccessible are those in quadrant 4 (written-external), since they could include a lengthy search process. Perhaps most inaccessible are sources in quadrant 1 (written-internal), because such sources have to be *produced* by the individuals in the organization.

This speculation is supported by earlier research by Peter G. Gerstberger and T. J. Allen. They found the single most important criterion used by research and development engineers in the selection of an information source to be the "law of least effort." Simply stated in terms of source selection, the law suggests that an individual selects the source that is most easily accessible and takes the least amount of work, or effort, to obtain. Perceived accuracy of the information source is a secondary consideration.[11] In a more recent study by O'Reilly, similar findings were produced: accessibility rather than perceived quality was the primary determinant of information selection.[12] Selection of informational input for decision situations in this study appears to follow the "law of least effort."

The perceived difficulty/importance of a decision situation does appear to modify the librarian's selection of an information source. However, this modification is subtle, and, at least in this study, only rarely does perceived difficulty/importance modify the selection process to include sources such as doing some research on my own or referring to statistical reports or internal studies produced by library staff. This attitude in decision making in the academic library has a number of implications.

Of primary importance is the consideration that for many libraries there simply are no internal or statistical reports. Obviously, if such sources are not available they cannot be selected. Furthermore, most librarians have neither the time nor the training to conduct internal analyses or do their own research. Many librarians have a hectic schedule that allows few blocks of time when production of information can take place. Moreover, few organizational rewards are available to those who invest their time in such a manner. And, finally, library schools have not trained professionals to be "researchers" in any practical sense of the word.

Because of the unavailability of such information, librarians are forced to rely on other information sources that can be described as "how we did it at our library." The professional literature abounds with this type of information, and other sources, such as oral ones, still largely provide information about how the decision was resolved in *one specific environment.* Although such information sources are useful, they can become extremely dangerous when used in excess because they cannot, by definition, take into consideration the specific environment unique to another library. Only internally produced reports and studies, or research, take these characteristics into consideration.

One likely result is that decisions are based on information appropriate for *other* organizations. What worked for one library may not work for another without acknowledgment of unique variables in that library environment. Yet, apparently, information sources unique to one environment are relied on wholesale for decisions at other library environments. Given such a process, librarians cannot be surprised to learn that what worked well at library X does not work well in "my" library. Until there are organizational information sources based on internal analyses and research, dependence on another library's experiences is likely to continue.

On a related matter, this lack of diversity of information sources selected for various decision situations encourages an information nepotism. This nepotism implies an inbreeding of "favorite" sources that provide a narrow, provincial view of the decision situation within the organization. This occurs on two levels. First, the information sources selected reinforce other similar sources. If a journal article is selected, the bibliography encourages the selection of another journal article. The same process is likely with an initial selection of an oral source. Second, the librarians, overall, prefer those sources encouraged by the law of least effort. The result of this phenomenon is that 80 percent of the selections come from 20 percent of the sources. This nepotism within the organization does not encourage the selection of information sources that have specific relevance and accuracy for the decision under consideration. Furthermore, a decision is unique to one library because it takes place in an environment that is, by definition, different from any other library's environment.

Another major implication of these findings related to the selection of information sources for specific decision situations has to do with planning. Planning is a process of identifying organizational goals and objectives, developing programs or services to accomplish those objectives, and evaluating the success of those programs vis-à-vis the stated objectives.[13] Organizational planning assumes the availability of information sources unique to that particular library. Typically, information resulting from a needs assessment, a community analysis, or another data collection technique emphasizes the *production* of information by organizational members. This kind of information is represented in this study as internal reports or statistical information and doing some research on my own.

The development of systematic and ongoing organizational planning is crucial for the effectiveness of the library both internally and externally. Internally, planning encompasses the entire span of organizational decision making, identifies program priorities, encourages rational resource allocation, and provides a framework of challenge and responsibility for all organizational members. Externally, planning provides a means to respond to environmental changes and suggests specific actions to satisfy the need of various user groups. Perhaps even more important, planning provides proof positive to the library's governing board(s) of rational decision making and organizational purpose.

Effective library planning is unlikely without an adequate base of information specifically related to the unique nature of an organization and its environment. However, the data from this study suggest minimal selection of such information as input for decision making. Apparently, little collection and analysis of organizational information is accomplished by libraries in this study; such information sources either are produced but not selected, not produced, or produced but available *only* to certain individuals. Most likely, a combination of the last two alternatives describes many library organizations.

Reasons for the nonproduction of organizational information in an academic library are numerous. However, as long as the law of least effort is operative in the selection of information sources, perceived value of information sources may be better understood by the perceived difficulty/importance of the decision. Such a theoretical approach is another method to describe perceived value of information without utility and non-utility categories.

Perceived Value = $f(E + I)$ where

1. f = function of individual's value system
2. E = law of least effort
3. I = perceived difficulty/importance of the decision situation

Such an approach is less complementary to our desire for a rational, logical explanation of perceived value of an information source to be selected for a specific decision situation. Nonetheless, it may be as accurate as or perhaps more accurate predictor of behavior than the utility model suggested at the beginning of this chapter.

Both models are suggested as heuristics for future research and no attempt has been made specifically to verify one or the other in this discussion. Data from this study do suggest that the intuitive or nonrational aspects of perceived value of information sources selected as input for decision making deserve greater attention from researchers. Although specific utility and non-utility characteristics may affect the law of least effort in part, the gestalt of the concept will be difficult to describe and quantify. In the harried life of academic library decision making, these concepts (the law of least effort and perceived difficulty/importance of the decision situation) may provide the basis for administrative strategies to improve the organizational contact and selection of information sources for decision making.

The key, of course, is the increased awareness on the part of library decision makers of the importance and benefits of managing and producing organizational information. The various administrative levels in the academic library do not appear to provide leadership in terms of information management, that is, the production, collection, organization, and dissemination of information within the organization. A proactive stance must be developed to manage information resources as a basis for improved decision making that will affect all services and operations within the library. Based on the findings presented in the two studies described, the importance of information management and strategies for its implementation will be discussed in the concluding chapter.

NOTES

1. Clare W. Graves, "Levels of Existence: An Open System Theory of Values," *Journal of Humanistic Psychology,* 10 (Fall 1970): 131-55.

2. Emanual Peterfreund, *Information, Systems, and Psychoanalysis* (New York: International Universities Press, 1971), p. 111.

3. B. A. Weisbod, "Comparing Utility Functions in Efficiency Terms," *American Economic Record,* 67 (December 1977): 991-95.

4. Roman R. Andrus, "Approaches to Information Evaluation," in *Readings in Management Information Systems,* ed. Gordon B. Davis and Gordon C. Everest (New York: McGraw-Hill, 1976), p. 103.

5. Ibid., p. 105.

6. Peter G. Gerstberger and T. J. Allen, "Criteria Used by Research and Development Engineers in the Selection of an Information Source," *Journal of Applied Psychology,* 52 (August 1968): 272-79.

7. Robert W. Zmud, "An Empirical Investigation of the Dimensionality of the Concept of Information," *Decision Science,* 9 (April 1978): 187-95.

8. Graham Jones, "This Incredible Stream of Garbage: The Library Journals 1876-1975," *The Indexer,* 10 (April 1976): 9-14.

9. Richard Trueswell, "Some Behavioral Patterns of Library Users: The 80/20 Rule," *Wilson Library Bulletin,* 43 (January 1969): 458-61.

10. Audrey Sylvia Tobias, "The Yule Curve, Describing Periodical Citations by Freshmen," *Journal of Academic Librarianship,* 1 (March 1975): 14-16.

11. Gerstberger and Allen, "Criteria Used by Research and Development Engineers in the Selection of an Information Source," p. 277.

12. Charles A. O'Reilly, III, "Variations in Decision Makers' Use of Information Sources: The Impact of Quality and Accessibility of Information," Berkeley: University of California, School of Business Administration, February 1979 (mimeograph).

13. Charles R. McClure, "The Planning Process: Strategies for Action," *College & Research Libraries,* 39 (November 1978): 456-66.

7
ORGANIZATIONAL INFORMATION MANAGEMENT

INFORMATION POTENTIAL

A major concern of this book has been to stress the importance of organizational members' contact with and evaluation of information for decision making. This emphasis is especially crucial if one accepts the assumption that every member of the organization is a decision maker, that is, each person must convert information into action on a daily basis in order to perform his or her job effectively. This conversion process, or a person's information potential, is largely determined by the person's ability to contact and select information sources related to organizational goals and objectives.

The differentiation between a decision maker and an administrator is also crucial. A typical misconception is that only administrators can be decision makers. Such may have been the case in years past, but an organization depends on the effectiveness of daily decisions made by all members. Indeed, in a service-oriented organization such as the library, the decisions made by employees working with the public (not administrators) have the most direct effect on user satisfaction. Therefore, stress is placed upon the notion that all members of the organization are decision makers; a few of these decision makers may also have administrative responsibility.

Finally, emphasis has been placed on the individual and the idea that human resources are the most important resources at the disposal of the organization. The human element is the critical link in the conversion of information into action; the human element determines the allocation of various support resources in the conversion process; and the human element ultimately is responsible for the accomplishment of goals and objectives. If an organization employs twenty individuals who are contributing to the accomplishment of goals at only 75 percent of their potential, there is a total loss of five positions in the organization.

Clearly, very few organizations can afford to "lose" one-quarter of their staff. Inefficient and ineffective contact with and selection of information sources ultimately affects each *individual* decision maker, not only *administrative* decision makers. In times of tight budgets, limited resources, and increased accountability, organizations must develop specific strategies to improve organizational information management. Such strategies rest upon the assumptions that all organizational members are decision makers, and human resources are the most important and typically the most underutilized resources in the library organization.

The concept of "information potential" was introduced as a means to examine an individual's contact with and selection of information broadly related to the accomplishment of the organization's goals and objectives. Contact with information sources may be seen as a reservoir of sources. The person maintains contact with such sources as a current awareness process in expectation that such sources will be useful in the performance of the job at some point in the future. Selection of information is decision specific, that is, information is selected as input to reduce the uncertainty surrounding a specific decision situation.

The concept of information potential is a key element for the effective management of organizational information resources. Further exploration of the concept may provide a basis on which (1) the relationship between information and decision making can be better understood, (2) the use of information in an organization can be examined, and (3) strategies for organizational information management can be developed. Based on these objectives, a model for the concept of information potential is presented in Figure 7-1.[1]

This model attempts to incorporate the major concepts that have been addressed throughout this volume. As such, it is a tentative view which will be useful if it assists researchers in their study of the information-decision process or if it assists decision makers in their development of strategies for improved utilization of human and information resources in the organization. The model should be viewed as one possible approach as opposed to a definitive view of the concept of information potential.

Information-handling ability can be described as the individual's information consciousness: that is, his or her philosophical stance on the importance of information sources in the decision process; awareness of the information environment related to the job, organization, and profession; and ability to both contact and select appropriate information sources for given decision situations. In short, information-handling ability attempts to describe the complex process by which the person matches and mixes elements among the other variables in the model.

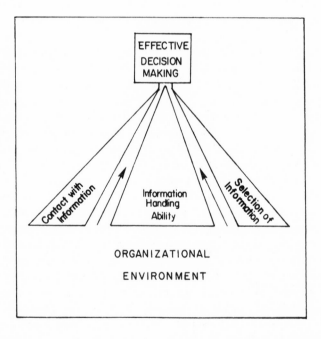

FIGURE 7-1   The Concept of Information Potential for Decision Making

Individual characteristics also play an important role in an individual's information-handling ability. Findings presented in this volume suggest that above average contact with information is necessary but not sufficient for involvement in decision making. Individual characteristics such as innate intelligence, personality traits, ability to interact with other individuals, ambition/motivation, and other factors related to cognition and affect may be considered here as well. Although the individual characteristics may be important determinants to overall information potential, the data presented in this volume suggest that information-related variables are likely to be of equal if not greater significance.

Contact with information and selection of information have been described in detail in this volume. The model stresses the close interaction between the two processes and further suggests that effective decisions result from *both* the selection and contact process. Although it is likely that some decision makers may tend to rely on one process more than the other, *effective* decisions are related to the individual's ability to use the two processes in a complementary, reinforcing fashion.

The organizational environment includes a host of possible elements. Clearly, such characteristics as the structure of the organization, the organizational climate, the use of various styles of management, and the allocation of resources within the organization must be considered. Additionally, a broader view of organizational environment that includes its interaction with nonorganizationally controlled characteristics such as clients or patrons and the larger societal context that affects the organization also may be considered. Finally, the concept of an organization's information environment may be considered here. The ability of the organization as a whole to encourage information resources management will affect an individual's information potential.

Ultimately, the product of these variables is effective information resource management for organizational decision making. The degree of mix and interaction among the variables for a group of individuals is likely to fluctuate considerably. However, effective decision making in this sense means decisions that accomplish the goals and objectives of the organization. Such a definition may suggest that analysis of the concept of information potential can be applied at both an individual and organizational level. Nonetheless, effective decision making—at least in terms of information potential—deserves careful attention as a means for improved organizational effectiveness and information resource management.

Obviously, more research will be required to test the model. Operational definitions and measures of the variables will not be either easy or simple. However, additional research along the lines suggested in this model may provide a basis for a predictive model that can be used to analyze information potential in an organizational setting. Improved information potential of both individuals and organizations is likely to be the administrative challenge of the future.

SUMMARY AND IMPLICATIONS

An examination of librarians' contact with information supports T. J. Allen's finding that certain people tend to contact more sources of information than other organizational members.[2] This investigation expands Allen's conclusion to include more traditional organizational structures such as an academic library as opposed to the rather specialized structure of the research and development setting that Allen investigated. In the setting of the academic library, librarians in specific categories, such as administrators, opinion leaders, and those involved in decision making, tend to contact substantially more information sources than other types of librarians.

Furthermore, the librarians on whom these administrators rely for informational input into the decision-making process also come into contact with a substantially greater number of factual information sources than the typical library employee. Opinion leaders, who are 100 percent involved in decision making, also tend to be organizational information rich. Thus, in the four libraries studied, decision making is both formally and informally done by those librarians who come into contact with a substantially larger quantity of factual information sources than other librarians in the organization.

In a recent Ph.D. dissertation, Robert Swisher studied the relationship of nine types of external information sources to independent variables such as career stability, educational attainment, publication activity, professional mobility, age, and years of professional experience. Although Swisher only studied academic librarians belonging to The American Library Association (ALA) and information sources that were external, and did not examine their relationship to decision making, his results support a number of findings from this investigation.

Swisher found, as did this researcher, that academic library administrators come into contact with more sources of information than either public or technical service librarians. However, he reported that contacts of public service and technical service librarians with information sources were virtually the same. That finding does not support the data from this research, which shows that public service librarians contact substantially more sources of information than technical service librarians. It may be suggested that the discrepancy is explained because his study sampled ALA members only, whereas this investigation sampled all librarians in a given library. One might speculate that membership in a professional organization is evidence, in itself, of an increased number of contacts with factual information.

Other findings from the Swisher study that support results from this investigation are: the librarian's number of contacts with factual information sources is not related to age; administrators contacted more information sources than nonadministrators; among academic librarians, publication was the exception and not the rule; and librarians who had engaged in some form of publication activity contacted more factual information sources than librarians who had not.[3]

The fact that a librarian is an administrator indicates that the larger governing body places more value on that librarian's ideas than on those of other librarians, and, if the librarian is an opinion leader, this is informal organizational evidence that other librarians place more value on that librarian's ideas than those of other librarians. Both these groups of librarians come into contact with substantially more information sources than the average librarian. This suggests that increased contact with information sources is related to involvement in decision making.

The librarian tends to be a generalist in terms of the types of factual information sources with which he or she comes into contact. This statement is supported by two methods of reasoning. Looking first at the various methods used in this investigation to classify librarians (by jobtype, organizational information richness, involvement in decision making, or sociometric type), no patterns of preferences for certain types of factual information emerge. The total number of contacts are relatively evenly spread among the sources of information—except for those related to publication activity.

A second line of reasoning focuses primary attention on categories of information sources instead of categories of libraries. Table 4-5 describes the average contacts with administrative/research sources and Table 4-7 describes the average contacts with internal/external sources. A comparison of the *total* contacts is meaningless because the two categories rely on different numbers of variables (information sources). What is meaningful is the relative balance of *selection* between either administrative/research sources or internal/external sources of factual information.[4]

Other researchers who have studied the factual information sources of professionals in an organizational setting generally emphasize external sources. Allen's concept of a "gatekeeper"[5] and Swisher's study of "cosmopolate" information sources[6] examine information sources that are largely external to the organization. Academic librarians in this investigation tend to come into contact with a wide diversity of information sources. No clear preferences for one type of information source are apparent. Organizational information richness appears to be the result of coming into contact with more *total* sources as opposed to increasing the contact with a selected type of factual information source.

Another implication that one may find in this investigation is that the jobtype or organizational position of the individual is related to his or her total contacts with information sources and perceived value of information sources selected. A review of the findings lends support to the idea that those librarians who have administrative responsibilities (regardless of title) believe such responsibilities require them to be more *informed* with factual information related to their position, organization, or profession. Other positions in the library may not *require* contact with additional sources of information for satisfactory performance.

Based on the definition used in this investigation that information resolves, reduces, or increases uncertainty, it can be assumed that the number of contacts with factual information sources is an indicator of the relative uncertainty associated with the performance of a given position type. Thus, the data suggest that administrators deal with more uncertainty in the performance of their position than do public service librarians, who in turn deal with more uncertainty than technical service librarians.

This line of reasoning implies that the position and job responsibilities may in part determine, or at least affect, the number of contacts and the various information selections a librarian might make. Such a notion is given support from organizational researchers studying motivation, who indicate that if a person has little need for information contact (the job does not require it) and/or the person does not receive some "reward" for additional information contact (recognition, promotion, salary increase), the individual simply will not seek contacts with information sources.[7]

An implication of this analysis of uncertainty involves the creativity of the individuals in the organization. Creativity may be considered the ability to ask new questions, regard problem situations from a new perspective, and to use imagination in the rearrangement of concepts. The relationship between information sources and creativity is crucial for organization effectiveness. Conrad Kasperson suggests that creative scientists acquire information differently from other scientists in three distinct ways:[8]

1. They had greater exposure to people in discipline areas outside their own area specialty.
2. They had greater contact with periodicals of original research.
3. Superiors as an information source were found most useful to the noncreative/nonproductive scientists and significantly less useful to the creative scientists.

Although an extrapolation of these results to information use characteristics of academic librarians is difficult, the results presented in this volume suggest that academic librarians:

1. have limited contact with individuals outside their immediate speciality in librarianship, to say nothing of contact with individuals outside librarianship
2. have little contact with periodicals that report original research
3. seek information primarily from their immediate supervisors.

The specific criteria suggested by Kasperson as indicators of creativity, in general, are not illustrative of academic librarians. Thus, their information use characteristics do not suggest an environment that encourages creativity and innovation.

Paradoxically, the analysis of general types of factual information based on A. G. Smith's classification of information sources as either administrative or research[9] lends support to Allen's differentiation of sources as internal or external to the organization. The use of factor analysis, which was performed on the various sources of factual information studied in this investigation, identified two factors that explained up to 65 percent of the total variance. An analysis of the variables being measured by these factors clearly indicates that the first factor measured internal sources and the second factor measured external sources of information. Thus, additional support is given to the notion that organizational information sources can be classified as either internal or external, as Allen has suggested.[10]

Recent research by Tagliacozzo suggests that when decision makers in public service institutions seek information for a specific decision situation, they prefer sources of information inside the organization and only infrequently seek information from external sources. That finding is supported by results of this investigation. When library directors identified the person on whom they most frequently relied for information pertaining to a given decision situation, only 22 percent of the people identified were external to the library organization.

A subjective analysis of those situations in which individuals outside the organization were selected also supports Tagliacozzo's finding that "external sources of information were used more often when the decision was 'very important' or 'extremely important' than when it was of lower importance."[11]

Although this finding can be explained largely by the greater accessibility of people (or sources) internal to the organization, there is another possible explanation. One might speculate that many of the decision situations affecting the academic libraries studied in this investigation were of "limited" or "minor" importance. This line of reasoning seems to suggest that many of the decisions in these libraries can be categorized—according to Herbert A. Simon—as "programmed," or repetitive and proceduralized decisions.[12]

In both contact with and selection of information sources, librarians utilize few, if any, internal reports or statistical analyses. Yet, those who do utilize such sources tend to be information rich and involved in decision making. The implications of this finding are substantial and suggest that there is little in-house production of information, limited planning, limited organizational research, and limited ability to cope effectively with environmental changes unique to that library.

A political implication of the study is that contact with information sources is related to involvement in decision making. Three different methods of analysis support this finding. The first method of analysis assured the identification of information rich librarians by defining the organizational information rich as those librarians who scored in the top 50 percent of total contacts with factual information sources. The relationship between this group of individuals (information rich) and involvement in decision making was statistically significant.

The second and third methods identified other groups of librarians who tended to be information rich. The relationship between administrators and information richness was statistically significant; the relationship between opinion leaders and information richness was also significant. It should be noted that these two groups were identified because of their formal position as administrators or because of their informal roles as opinion leaders. In either case, group membership was determined by *organizational position,* not by the researcher. However, the relationship of administrators or opinion leaders to involvement in decision making is significant.

Three group types—organizational information rich, administrators, and opinion leaders—contact substantially more sources of factual information than other librarians and all three groups show significant relationships with involvement in decision making. These three methods of analysis provide strong support for the hypothesis that those people who are identified as the organizational information rich in an academic library tend to be involved in library decision making. Based on these findings, one might speculate that variables such as leadership and political power also are likely to be related to contact with information.

However, organizational information richness is necessary but not sufficient to be involved in decison making. This finding reinforces the idea that factual information sources are only part, albeit a significant part, of the broad range of resources that might be utilized as input in the decision-making process. Such phenomena as individual cognition, the person's abilities, and the complex personality characteristics of the individual are also likely to be related to involvement in decision making.

An implication of this finding is that, by and large, librarians investigated are not rational decision makers, at least in terms according to

Simon's definition. For a decision to be "rational" it must meet the following two criteria: (1) it must be a choice among alternatives, and (2) it must attempt to accomplish a stated objective.[13] Other researchers, most notably Chris Argyris, severely criticize Simon's emphasis on man as a rational decision maker, even in terms of bounded rationality.[14]

Based on individual comments received during the various interviews as well as the actual data, the decision-making process in these libraries does not meet Simon's two criteria for rational decision making. Typically, decisions are made by the ebb and flow of power politics, by administrative fiat, with little factual data as input, and with no clearcut objective for the intended outcome of the decision. Further research is necessary to study overall effectiveness of rational decision making versus "irrational" decision making in library organizations. However, the subjective view of this writer is that academic libraries have much room to improve their organizational information management for rational decision making.

The sociometric analysis of information-seeking patterns in the library identified opinion leaders, all of whom were involved in decision making and information rich. Allen also identified sociometric stars who act as gatekeepers of technical information flow within the research and development organization.[15] The characteristics of these gatekeepers are similar to the characteristics of the opinion leaders identified in this study in that they both have more contacts with such sources as professional literature and friends outside the organization. This investigation also supports the conclusions of Farace and Danowski that "liaisons" (another type of organizational information rich reported in the literature) are more likely to serve as first sources of information, have higher formal status in the organization, and have levels of education and age similar to those of other members.[16] The specific information contacts that separate these individuals from others are greater contact with external sources and greater contact with internal statistical reports or other studies. But patterns of information seeking tended to follow formal lines of authority and little cross-departmental information seeking was identified.

This lack of cross-departmental information seeking has also been identified in a public library environment. In a dissertation by C. N. Kies, one finding was that many librarians named first their immediate supervisor and then their supervisor's supervisor as primary sources for information seeking. Such a finding not only provides "more orientation toward a few individuals high in the hierarchy but [also shows] definite reinforcement of that hierarchy."[17] The implication, of course, is that information flow is poorly organized, which limits creativity, innovation, and change and increases the bureaucratic nature of the library.

Those librarians who contact substantial information sources appear to be much more adept in their ability to affect the library's political process. Based on number of information contacts, librarians may be categorized as recluse, technician, politician, or zealot. Generally, librarians in this study tend to manifest information contact characteristics similar to those described for technicians. Librarians are as likely to be recluses as politicians in their information contacts and only a few tend to be described as zealots.

Thus, an implication of this investigation is that there may be a point where a librarian's increased contacts with information sources may become less useful to the organization as a whole. "Useful" to the organization is evidenced when the information sources are integrated into decision making or other members of the organization seek information from those people who come into contact with more factual information sources than others. This concept can be termed as information overload: the librarian comes into contact with so many factual information sources that they cannot be utilized effectively by the organization. The concept is characterized by the zealot.

Inevitably, then, one returns to the relationship between quantity of information and quality of performance. Although one implication of this study is that there may be a break point beyond which additional contact with factual information sources is of decreasing usefulness to the organization, there is another, equally important implication that having above average contacts with factual information sources is necessary for the librarian to be an administrator, involved in decision making, or an opinion leader.

The seemingly contradictory relationship between these two implications can be explained by Figure 7-2. Increasing one's contact with factual information sources may be related directly to the individual's quality of performance only up to a certain level, at which point information overload takes place and increased contact with information sources is either nonproductive or perhaps dysfunctional. Other researchers have suggested

such a relationship between information sources and their effect on performance, but largely outside the organizational decision-making framework of analysis.[18]

Thus, there appears to be a positive relationship between quantity of
factual information contacts with quality of individual performance (assuming that being an administrator or an opinion leader is prima facie
evidence of quality performance). Such a conclusion is speculative, and
Figure 7-2 explains, at best, only part of the relationship between quantity
of information and quality of performance. The second part of the relationship involves variables related to individual cognition, personality
characteristics, organizational power/politics, and other factors related
to affect. As this investigation suggests, contact with a larger number of
factual information sources is necessary, but not sufficient to be involved
in decision making (one indicator of organizational performance). However, Figure 7-2 presents one possible method by which the relationship
between quantity of sources and quality of performance can be described.

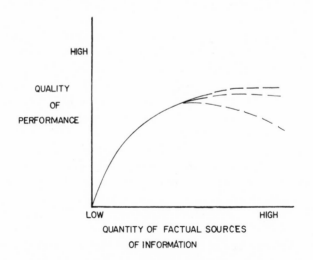

FIGURE 7-2   Relationship between Quantity of Factual
Information and Quality of Performance

During the *selection* of information sources as input for a specific decision situation, data from this study suggest that a few sources tend to account for a vast majority of selections. Indeed, approximately 80 percent of the selection requirements are satisfied by 20 percent of the information sources. The implication of this finding is that little diversity of sources tends to increase the parochial and limited view of possible alternatives for a given decision situation. Furthermore, limited reliance on internally produced studies and reports suggests that information input is not geared to the unique environments of specific library situations.

The deeper one probes into this notion, the more paradoxical and disturbing the implications become. A systems view of the organization suggests that without feedback and information from the environment entropy and death are likely to occur.[19] The paucity of internally produced reports and studies suggests there is little analysis of the internal environment of the library itself, and the effect of decisions on society at large. This failure to adequately analyze environmental impacts of library decisions may contribute to the increasing development of nonlibrary information services in our country.[20]

The consideration that, overall, there is little difference among administrative jobtypes in perceived value of information sources selected for specific decision situations is also somewhat paradoxical. On one hand, administrators might be expected to show significantly different selection patterns since they are largely responsible for the decisions affecting the library—however, they do not. On the other hand the lack of differences among various administrative types speaks for a "democratic" or egalitarian approach to information selection for specific decision situations. However, the egalitarian stance of information selection is paradoxical in light of administrators' great *contact* with information sources. Training of information professionals in organizational information handling appears to be one necessary approach.

The general parochial view on the selection of information sources is further extenuated by the informal barriers that effectively remove women from involvement in the decision-making process. Although women tend to contact fewer information sources than men, they tend to select the same sources as men for input to specific decision situations. In the sample studied, approximately half of the information rich were women, but only 25 percent were involved in decision making, only 20 percent were opinion leaders, and women perceived their informational impact on decision making to be substantially less than men perceived their impact to be.

Possible reasons and excuses for the banning of women from decision making in academic libraries are many and complex. However, the implications of this situation are that a vast majority of professional librarians (namely women) are not contributing ideas, innovations, changes, or impact to the administrative direction of the organization. Such a fact reduces the feedback from a large "environment" of the library and increases the likelihood of parochialism, "good old boy" information networks, and, ultimately, entropy of the organization.

The "law of least effort" regarding information source selection is a key point to be addressed. The assumption that learning takes place because of feedback and evaluation during the selection of information sources deserves more attention. Because 80 percent of all information selections are satisfied by only 20 percent of the possible sources, one interpretation (an optimistic one) is that through previous learning, librarians have identified a small pool of possible sources that are perceived as valuable for a broad range of decision situations. However, another view (a pessimistic one) is simply that the "law of least effort" is responsible for the nondiversity of sources.

Regardless of which point of view is taken, the description of decision situations based on selection of information sources suggests that another factor should be considered. Figure 6-3 suggests a pattern by which the relative difficulty/importance of a decision situation affects the selection of certain categories of information sources. It is notable, however, that in no case did the perceived difficulty/importance of a decision situation reflect an overall selection of perhaps the most difficult source to access, written-internal, or sources that must be *produced* by the librarians themselves.

One might speculate that this finding suggests the limited knowledge and understanding of the complex decisions facing many academic librarians. Although the amount of change affecting academic libraries is large, the strategies of information input for those resulting decisions are limited. Basically, the selection of information revolves around two basic strategies: (1) check the professional literature, and (2) ask a colleague. The high dependence on these two strategies suggest that many librarians have limited appreciation for the complexity and impact of the decisions being made and the importance of producing information sources unique to the decision situation under consideration. The obvious result of this attitude is limited formalized planning of organizational activities and decreased organizational effectiveness.

This brief overview of major findings and implications resulting from the investigation suggests some situations in the academic library that are obvious, surprising, controversial, and at times paradoxical. Yet, the brunt of the message simply is that academic libraries and the librarians who work in them have failed to develop effective methods of organizational information handling. At both the organizational and individual level, contact with and selection of information sources for purposes of decision making can be improved. Methods to increase the information potential of organizational members must be devised if improved decision making in the academic library is to be accomplished.

STRATEGIES FOR ORGANIZATIONAL INFORMATION MANAGEMENT

THE NEED

Our administrative ability to operate effectively a service-oriented organization, such as an academic library, will depend in no small part upon our ability to marshal various information sources to resolve complex decision situations. Organizational information management, that is, the production, collection, organization, and dissemination of information related to the accomplishment of the organization's goals, should be encouraged. Organizational information management attempts to utilize the information resources of organizational members to full potential. Such an administrative stance is likely to improve the organization's access to both quantitative and qualitative information as well as improve the organization's ability to interact effectively with its environment.

The need for increased attention to organizational information handling is evidenced by recent societal changes. Office overhead is 30 to 50 percent of total costs in many business organizations; however, office productivity has increased only about 70 percent during the last century while factory productivity has increased by 1000 percent.[21] These figures are better understood when one considers that the average blue collar worker is supported by $30,000 worth of equipment, the farm worker by $55,000 worth of equipment, and the office worker by only $2,000 worth of equipment.[22] The librarian, as a typical office worker, simply has not been supported to increase his or her information-handling ability. Although better utilization of new technology is clearly needed in many libraries, the central problem is one of recognizing the importance of organizational information management.

Strategies can be developed in the organization to better manage, acquire, and utilize information for decision making. However, a number of assumptions must be recognized by the organization before specific strategies can be developed and implemented. A first crucial assumption that must be met is that the organization is willing to change. Clearly, some of the strategies will rely on changing existing attitudes, administrative structures, and other existing techniques in the organization.

A second key assumption has to do with the administrative structure of the organization. Effective strategies for improved information handling will depend, in large part, on the managerial techniques and organizational climate in the library. As previously pointed out, effective utilization of information in the organization is based on the ideas that (1) every employee is a decision maker, and (2) the most important resource of the organization is the individual. Appropriate administrative strategies may have to be developed first to integrate these concepts into the library *before* strategies for organizational information handling can be successfully developed.

CONTINGENCY MANAGEMENT STYLES

A primary need that can be identified for successful information management is the development of management styles and organizational climates that respond individually to unique situations to maximize goal attainment. Such styles must provide input and feedback from the library's environment, recognize the importance of rational decision making, and facilitate the contact, selection, and dissemination of information to all organizational members. Furthermore, these contingency styles of management must provide clear evidence of administrative accountability by decentralizing the control over organizational sources of information.

Typically, such contingency views recognize the potential for various shared decision-making styles. These management styles assume that employees are both willing and able to contribute to the decision-making process if they are adequately informed by administration and if they assume responsibility for contacting adequate information sources and selecting accurate and relevant information sources for decision making. All organizational members assume the responsibility for developing organizational structures to encourage shared decision making as well as the decentralization of information sources.

The term "shared decision making" is used to indicate more of a concept of management than a specific technique such as MBO. Shared decision making implies a process of power equalization in the organization, with administration encouraging informational input into the decision-making process and sharing responsibility for the consequences resulting from the decision with those who were involved in making the decision. Participation is a type of shared decision making and involves all members of the organization or all stakeholders in a given decision situation who provide informational input but who do not necessarily assume responsibility for the consequences of the decision.[23]

Librarians wishing to move their organization toward shared decision-making managerial styles must first recognize the importance of key information-related variables such as (1) the individual's access to organizational information sources, (2) the individual's contact with organizational information sources, (3) the individual's selection of sources as input for decision making, and (4) the informal dissemination of information within the organization. Further, it may be suggested that ignorance of the importance of these key variables largely explains the failure of many shared decision-making management styles in a number of library organizations.

Effective organizational information management appears to be a prerequisite for the various shared decision-making styles. Furthermore, a period of preparation in which information-related variables are modified also appears to be a prerequisite for shared decision-making styles. Superimposing management styles on library environments where information contact, flow, and availability are minimal often may result in a self-fulfilling prophecy of doom for the new style. Organizational information management has not been recognized as an important determinant of the introduction and change of management styles.

Furthermore, the question of responsibility must be raised. Does the administrator have a responsibility to encourage professional librarians to come into contact with information sources? The answer appears to be yes if he or she is trying to move the organization to a more shared decision-making style of management. Do professional librarians have a responsibility to come into contact with more information sources and facilitate the flow of information within the organization? The answer appears to be yes if they wish to become involved in decision making and make participatory styles of management more effective.

REDUCE PROGRAMMED DECISION SITUATIONS

A specific strategy that can be employed to encourage contact with information sources is to reduce the degree to which "programmed" decisions are determining employee activity. Job satisfaction and increased productivity appear to be likely when professionals have new challenges to address—challenges for which increased contact with information sources provides a basis for the individuals to develop their potential as decision makers. Administrators as well as other individuals must strive to include "non-programmed" decision situations in their environment. From such situations comes the need for unique or new information that may provide the basis for innovation and change.

One method to reduce the degree to which librarians deal only with programmed decisions is to encourage their contact with decision situations outside their immediate department. Because employees in an organization receive more information related to their immediate work environment than information related to the organization as a whole,[24] strategies should be employed to provide the employee with a broader view of the organization. Such a strategy not only increases the employee's contact with nonprogrammed decision situations but also encourages the employee to relate the needs and objectives of various organizational parts to each other.

For the most part, the research suggests that librarians are not educated consumers of information; a need exists for librarians to learn how to evaluate information as potential input to decision making. A strategy that can be employed to respond to this need is reeducation. Specifically, the central points to be addressed are (1) explanation of the importance of information input in the decision-making process, (2) accepting as a professional responsibility to be informed and current vis-à-vis matters affecting the organization, (3) learning how to achieve access effectively to the broad array of information sources that have potential input to organizational decision making, and (4) developing the ability to critically evaluate the information one contacts or selects as to its "value" for decision making. Reeducation is necessary if programmed decision making is to be reduced.

EDUCATION ABOUT INFORMATION HANDLING

Reeducation of librarians about information management can be addressed at two levels. The first level is that of students currently obtaining their professional training in library/information science. Traditional library science management courses of an historical nature which begin with scientific management and conclude with systems management cannot be the student's only contact with organizational information management. The process of information handling in the organizational setting must be presented along with the various strategies of organizational information management.

Indeed, the usefulness of organizational information management is not limited to library/information science students. Conversations with various professionals in other disciplines suggest that most professional graduates from institutions of higher education are unprepared to effectively utilize the various information sources in their fields, to contribute information to the organizational decision-making process, or to organize and control their personal information-related activities in an organizational setting. Producing professionals of any type who are unable to cope with the realities of the information society is a disservice both to the individuals and to society at large.

There is some evidence that educators are recognizing the need for such informational training. A recent publication, *Evaluating Information: A Guide for Users of Social Science Research,* attempts to educate students, regardless of discipline, to be consumers of information.[25] The assumption of the work is that all professionals must be able to assess the accuracy and appropriateness of the mass of research findings currently being produced. This is an excellent strategy to integrate into various courses at both the graduate and the undergraduate level. Students exposed to this strategy are more likely to have increased information potential in the organization where they ultimately work, regardless of their specific job responsibilities.

A second level of educating must be accomplished for those professionals already in the field. The amount of work that must be done here
is staggering. The data in this study suggest that many librarians are in-
adequately prepared to contact and select information sources for decision making. Currently, there is growing pressure for professionals to
improve their information-handling techniques. However, future demands for accountability and justification of decisions will force the
librarian to be better informed, more selective, and more aware of organizational information management techniques.

Three strategies are possible at this level. First, library educators
must assume responsibility for reeducating professionals in the field,
and the profession at large must accept the need for some type of an
ongoing certification program to *insure* that librarians improve their
capacity for current developments and better information management.
Such strategies are already accepted in the professions of medicine,
education, law, and dentistry. Paradoxically, the professions of library/
information science do not *require* their professional members to attend a designated number of instructional programs after completion of
the initial degree.

Second, library administrators must assume responsibility for information management training programs. This strategy would contribute
to the decentralization of information control as well as provide a laboratory environment for the development of organizational information managerial skills. Specific techniques for improving the organization's contact with information, production of information, and dissemination of information can be fostered in this manner. Library administrators must provide the opportunity for in-house training sessions;
they must encourage staff participation in the sessions; and they must assume responsibility for providing leaders for those sessions who are knowledgeable about organizational information management.

Third, the development of training manuals, procedures, and other
guides is an excellent first step toward improved information resource
management. Such guides can be developed to fit the specific needs
of an organization and can aid in the transition from manual information
handling to automated information handling. Such a strategy helps to
insure appropriate information flows within the organization and can
encourage decentralization of information. A number of these guides
have been produced by organizations in government and the business

world and provide useful models for the library environment.[26] Furthermore, there are a number of recent books that provide an excellent basis for analyzing and developing information resources in the organization.[27] Examination of such books can be a positive first step in readying the organization for procedures, changes, and new strategies vis-à-vis improved information handling.

THE INFORMATION MANAGER

Throughout the research there is evidence that no one has overall responsibility for organizational information management in the library environment. This need can be addressed by establishing authority and responsibilities to improve organizational information handling. Although there is no lack of "administrators," the appreciation of information contact, information dissemination, and information selection for decision making is not recognized as a responsibility either for administrators or for librarians in general.

The job title "information manager" is becoming much more common in a number of businesses as well as in government sectors. Specific responsibilities for the information manager include the following:

1. Direct the overall development of information resources for improved organizational decision making.
2. Coordinate the organization's access to and dissemination of information related to the accomplishment of goals and objectives.
3. Facilitate the exchange of organizational information among organizational members.
4. Organize the production of analytical information related to the organization's interaction with the environment for purposes of planning.
5. Provide a storage and retrieval system for information resources related to the organization's operations and services.
6. Evaluate existing mechanisms of information access and dissemination and propose alternative methods by which organizational members will have access to information resources for decision making.

These responsibilities must be clearly assigned to one individual in the organization, preferably an administrator.

The designated individual must have broad skills and knowledge of information sciences, information technology in all its various formats, personnel and social psychology, contingency management techniques, systems analysis and program planning, and at least basic statistical skills for summary and analysis of information. Such an individual is a broker or counselor who acts as a facilitator between information resources and organizational decision making. "Perhaps above all else the information manager is a resource manager . . . to enhance, and conserve information resources to help the organization achieve its lawful goals and objectives."[28]

Specific strategies that can be utilized by the information manager to accomplish the responsibilities of the position are many and are limited only by one's imagination. Indeed, many of the strategies that have been successfully utilized in the business world such as (1) project management, (2) brainstorming sessions, (3) selective dissemination of information for company professionals, (4) creation of an information resource center, and (5) training sessions on how to improve one's information potential are most appropriate for the service sector such as academic libraries.[29] Until such strategies are implemented we will continue to lose the full potential of our professionals as decision makers.

The information manager may also serve as a means to respond to another need clearly identified in this study—the nonproduction of information in the form of reports, studies, and statistical analyses. Libraries must initiate responsibility for institutional research—research that deals with both the internal operations and services of the library and the library's impact on and relationship with its environment. The production of unique information that addresses specific aspects of the library and its environment is crucial for improved organizational decision making.

However, the purpose of the position is not to centralize further the control of information in the organization. Because all professionals are decision makers, special emphasis should be placed on extending access to information resources throughout the organization. As such, the individual also serves as an advisor to the staff on how to utilize information sources for daily decision making. The assumption that only top administration needs adequate access to and control of information resources must be challenged. The decentralization of information resources encourages all staff members to develop their full potential as organizational decision makers, a potential which appears to be largely untapped in many academic libraries today.

DECENTRALIZATION OF INFORMATION

In a general sense, decentralization of information can be encouraged by restructuring various task responsibilities. As shown in this study, many typical positions in the library environment have little uncertainty associated with their performance. Yet, recent research suggests that tasks perceived as more uncertain will be associated with more frequent use of information sources.[30] Thus a strategy of restructuring various librarian positions to include responsibility for nonprogrammed decisions (ones in which there is some uncertainty) will tend to encourage information acquisition and organizational decentralization of information.

The concept of organizational power (discussed in chapter 5) is closely related to control of information and, thus, the centralization of information. When administrators maintain tight controls over the organization and dissemination of information, they also create a power base because the information can be used to reduce organizational uncertainties.[31] Although an advantage is maintained by administrators in terms of organizational control, the disadvantage of not utilizing the full potential of organizational employees is severe.

Nonetheless, given the magnitude of the information environment in which the typical librarian finds himself, administrators only can control *internally*-generated information. As pointed out previously in this study, the typical academic library studied produced very little such information. Thus, the librarian can clearly increase/improve the quality of his or her contacts with externally generated information. Furthermore, one should note that it is the externally generated information that tends to be "reality-bound," to provide greater validity than much internally generated information.[32]

Access to externally generated information provides a basis for a validity check, or perhaps a discrepancy check, between activities in the organization and its environment with the decision process within the organization. Therefore, one broad approach to limiting administrative control of information is consciously to acquire and disseminate externally generated information into the organization. Such an approach is especially useful when the discrepancy between internal activities and decisions do not match the evidence or information from the environment at-large.

Decentralization of information can be accomplished by a number of strategies. One approach is to maintain an open file system whereby all organizational memos, correspondence, reports, and so on are organized for employee availability. Another approach is to circulate summary data in the form of annual or quarterly reports from the various department heads throughout the organization. Furthermore, individuals in the organization can be assigned to a project group to study and make a report on certain decision situations, the results of which are circulated. Informal "group think" sessions and designated periods of time when administrators must report and be questioned on "current happenings" also can be set up. And, finally, librarians must learn to exchange information outside their specific departmental area; informal meetings can be established to do this.

Decentralization of information dissemination must also occur at the departmental level. As this research has shown, librarians tend to seek information from the immediate department supervisor. Such communication networks should be modified to encourage cross-departmental communication as well as integrating communication isolates into various communication networks in the library. Manipulation of membership in these communication networks may tend to significantly increase accuracy of information flow, creativity and problem-solving ability, as well as increase the coordination among the various departments. Inclusion of certain opinion leaders or information rich in specific network situations also may contribute to greater effectiveness of organizational information resource management.

However, the response of "forming a committee" may not always be a viable approach. The proliferation of committees does not necessarily equal decentralization of information. Committee structure is most effective *after* decentralization of information. Individuals must have access to organizational information before a meeting takes place so that meaningful analysis is possible. Agendas, provision of information related to the agenda items, and position papers encourage a dynamic environment of information exchange as a basis for committee effectiveness.[33]

REDUCING INFORMATION NEPOTISM

The disturbing aspect of nonproduction of information and its resulting information nepotism is that it does not encourage, but in fact generally precludes, the selection of information sources that have specific relevance and applicability to the specific decision under consideration. Thus, the very sources that are unique to the decision affecting the organization generally are ignored. If it is true, as it appears to be, that decision makers select and utilize a few fondly remembered information sources regardless of the problem at hand, the efficacy of the decisions is, at least, questionable.

Administrators can reduce information nepotism by encouraging the production of internal studies, reports, and statistical summaries. They should attempt to train, retrain, and promote basic writing and research skills. They should insist on empirical evidence as a basis for decisions whenever possible. They must expand their contact with and selection of information sources to those approximating the unique conditions in their library. They must encourage others in the organization to analyze the nature of the decision in terms of clearly defined objectives, establish alternatives, and evaluate alternatives based on clearly identified criteria. Finally, they must recognize the need for cross-departmental communication patterns and develop strategies to increase nonprogrammed decision situations for individual librarians.

Other decision makers (librarians) in the organization must critically examine the process by which they make decisions. What specific information resources (if any) were considered as input to the decision situation? How valuable were the information sources that were selected to resolve the decision situation? What patterns of informal information seeking were pursued? Did you *produce* information as a means of resolving the decision situation? How did you obtain critical feedback on the reliability and validity of the information contacted? How will you diversify your access to a broad range of information sources and increase your contact with those sources especially appropriate for your decision-making responsibilities.

Although these suggestions may be appropriate for administrators as well as librarians, the overall problem of information nepotism and the limited production of information resources must be addressed by all organizational members. Librarians might be organized into project teams to produce certain documents related to organizational activities and decisions. Such a strategy improves cross-departmental communication, increases the likelihood of creativity and innovation, and allows for the project team to be dissolved once the task is accomplished. Throughout this process, administration must encourage an organizational climate that supports access to information, production of information, and decentralization of information.

At present, individuals have not examined the information acquisition, processing, and dissemination characteristics of the people in the organization and, therefore, do not know who tends to be information rich, who tends to rely on other organization members who are information rich, or who relies on organization members with very low information potential as measured in that organization. The actual involvement of employees who might be termed organizational information rich within the decision-making process is little appreciated; indeed, self and organizational analysis of information processing is virtually nonexistent.

Those individuals who can be identified as information rich should be encouraged by the information manager to facilitate information handling in the organization. Perhaps special consideration should be shown to such organizational information rich employees in terms of allocation of information-related resources. External contacts with other professionals at conferences, meetings, and other occasions could be encouraged. Physical arrangements could be made to take advantage of the organizational information rich's expertise by placing them in easily accessible situations or where they could have more accessibility to prime information sources. Furthermore, communication networks in the organization could be studied to determine sources of information, exchange sequences, and relationships with other organizational employees.

Indeed, the whole question of resource allocation vis-à-vis information resources should be reexamined. Because information must be utilized *in conjunction with other resources* to be effective, administrators must examine the resources available to organizational members that encourage information exploitation. A long-distance call that costs $12.00 may in fact save the organization hundreds of dollars in other resources! Availability of time to examine and produce information also is a prerequisite, as well as information-handling equipment such as text editors, computers, and even telephones. Once the staff member has more self-determination regarding resources such as time, space, status, money, and equipment, he or she can better exploit information resources through other traditional resources and ultimately increase their information potential to the organization.

EVALUATING FOR INFORMATION POTENTIAL

Because a number of librarians (including administrators) appear not to appreciate the importance of information-related variables, performance evaluation of individuals based on their information potential may provide a useful stimulus for improved organizational information management. Evidence in the area of information performance evaluation is limited, but a recent study of interpersonal communication in a formal organization by Roberts and O'Reilly concluded that "both the quantity and quality of information [contacted by the employee] appear to be important correlates of individual performance *across a variety of tasks and functions*" (author's emphasis).[34] In another paper these two authors write that "the ability to obtain information is directly related to individual and group performance."[35] Information resources clearly are critical determinants for overall organizational effectiveness.

Managers in research and development organizations are being urged to evaluate employees on such criteria as "information potential," that is, the individual's ability to possess more and better information and to make the information more accessible to his or her colleagues. Winfred Holland suggests that "potential employees should be evaluated on their IP [information potential] as well as their personal productivity," to achieve maximum information transfer into the organization.[36] Allen's concern that management must recognize the importance of an individual's "information potential" is being acknowledged for research and development organizations, but the concept appears to have made little advancement in literature related to the management of public service institutions, such as libraries.

The notion of evaluation and performance measures of employees' information activity—contacts with factual information sources, interpersonal contacts, and dissemination of information to other organizational members—clearly deserves more attention in the organization. Traditional evaluation methods either of personality characteristics or ability to accomplish predetermined goals may be ignoring important determinants of organizational effectiveness when information activity is not considered. Additional attention to the individual's information potential through performance evaluation may be a most effective strategy to improve organizational information management.

THE ADMINISTRATIVE CHALLENGE

If one believes, as do many reputable scientists, that information is the ultimate frontier,[37] professionals in many organizational settings such as an academic library can look forward to an administrative challenge of significant magnitude. Paradoxically, librarians, who are information specialists, exhibit limited skills in organizational information management. The advent of microtechnology in computers, imagery, and other information-handling techniques for administrative purposes is but an image on the horizon for many public service institutions. Indeed, the vast armada of new information technologies has caused one information scientist to ask, "Whither libraries, or, wither libraries?"[38] Currently, our administrative use of information to make effective decisions appears to be tied into the "withering" process.

The realizations coming from a post-industrial society engaged in a true information revolution have raised considerable interest for improved information management and organizational decision making. And in the face of needed information support systems for administrative purposes, little significant progress has been made in libraries. Man's limited information-handling ability must be supported by new technologies including the computer. However, a prerequisite for such support systems is administration's awareness of the importance of information-related variables for improved organizational decision making.

Increased demands have been placed on administrators to justify their operations and increase the effectiveness of their organization. Academic libraries, as other types of public institutions, have not been excluded from such demands. It may be suggested that future strategies for improved organizational effectiveness will rely largely on process, or managerial solutions, rather than input, or increased levels of funding, staffing, and other resources. The marshalling of information-related resources will increase the administrator's responses as well as his or her ability to cope with rapid change. As this volume has suggested, the administrative challenge will be centered on the effectiveness of organizational information management and the administrator's ability to increase the information potential of individuals within the organization. Better utilization and integration of information and human resources may be our single best strategy for improved overall library effectiveness.

NOTES

1. This model is based, in part, on a model developed by Homer J. Hall, "Values in the Evaluation of Information" (mimeograph distributed by the author at the American Society for Information Science Annual Meeting, New York, November 1978).

2. T. J. Allen and S. I. Cohen, "Information Flow in Research and Development Laboratories," *Administrative Science Quarterly*, 14 (March 1969): 12-14.

3. Robert Dean Swisher, *Professional Communication Behavior of Academic Librarians Holding Membership in the American Library Association* (Ph.D. diss., University of Indiana, 1975).

4. Charles R. McClure, "Categories of Information Sources and Library Decision Making," in *The Information Age in Perspective: Proceedings of the ASIS Annual Meeting, 1978,* comp. Everett H. Brenner (White Plains, N.Y.: Knowledge Industries, 1978), pp. 213-16.

5. Allen, "Information Flow in Research and Development Laboratories," pp. 12-14.

6. Swisher, *Professional Communication Behavior of Academic Librarians.*

7. A. H. Maslow, "A Theory of Human Motivation," *Psychological Review,* 50 (1943): 270-96; Frederick Hersberg, *Work and the Nature of Man* (Cleveland, Ohio: World Publishing Company, 1966).

8. Conrad J. Kasperson, "An Analysis of the Relationship Between Information Sources and Creativity in Scientists and Engineers," *Human Communication Research,* 4 (Winter 1978): 118.

9. A. G. Smith, *Communication and Status: The Dynamics of a Research Center* (Eugene: University of Oregon, Center for the Advanced Study of Educational Administration, 1966).

10. Allen, "Information Flow in Research and Development Laboratories," pp. 12-18.

11. Renata Tagliacozzo, Manfred Kochen, and William Everett, "The Use of Information by Decision Makers in Public Service Organizations," in *Communication for Decision Makers: Proceedings of the American Society for Information Science,* ed. Jeanne B. North (Westport, Conn.: Greenwood Press, 1971), pp. 53-57.

12. Herbert A. Simon, *The New Science of Management Decision,* rev. ed. (Englewood Cliffs, N.J.: Prentice Hall, 1977), pp. 45-49.

13. Herbert A. Simon, *Administrative Behavior,* 3rd ed. (New York: The Free Press, 1976), pp. xxvi-xxxi.

14. Chris Argyris, "Some Limitations of Rational Man Organization Theory," *Public Administration Review,* 33 (May-June 1973): 253-67.

15. Allen, "Information Flow in Research and Development Laboratories," pp. 12-28.

16. Richard V. Farace and James A. Danowski, *Analyzing Human Communication Networks in Organizations, Applications to Management Problems* (East Lansing: Michigan State University, Department of Communication, 1973), ERIC Document no. 099943.

17. C. N. Kies, *Unofficial Relations, Personal Reliance, Informal Influence, Communication, and Library Staff: A Sociometric Investigation of Three Medium-Sized Public Libraries* (Ph.D. diss., Columbia University, 1977).

18. Karlene H. Roberts and Charles A. O'Reilly, III, *Interpersonal Communication, Personnel Ratings, and Systematic Performance Characteristics in Organizations* (Berkeley: University of California, Institute of Industrial Relations, 1975), NTIS Document no. AD A013874/7GA.

19. Fremont E. Kast and James E. Rosenzweig, "General Systems Theory: Applications for Organization and Management," *Academy of Management Journal,* 15 (December 1972): 447-68.

20. Marc Uri Porat, *The Information Economy,* 7 vols. (Washington, D.C.: U. S., Department of Commerce, 1977).

21. Frank Greenwood, "Your New Job in Information Management Resource," *Journal of Systems Management,* 30 (April 1979): 24.

22. Milton Rutherbusch, "Information Management in the Modern Automated Office," *Information & Records Management* (April 1979): 28.

23. Charles R. McClure, "Academic Librarians, Information Sources, and Shared Decision Making," *Journal of Academic Librarianship* 6 (March 1980): 9-15.

24. Gerald M. Goldhaber et al., "Organizational Communication: 1978," *Human Communication Research,* 5 (Fall 1978): 90-91.

25. Jeffrey Katzer, Kenneth H. Cook, and Wayne W. Crouch, *Evaluating Information: A Guide for Users of Social Science Research* (Reading, Mass.: Addison-Wesley, 1978).

26. U. S., Federal Paperwork Commission, *Reference Manual for Program and Information Officials,* 2 vols. (Washington, D.C.: U. S. Government Printing Office, 1978).

27. Forest W. Horton, Jr., *How to Harness Information Resources: A Systems Approach* (Cleveland, Ohio: Association for Systems Management, 1974).

28. Forest Woody Horton, Jr., "A Government Occupational Standard for Information Manager," *Information Manager,* 1 (March-April 1979): 34-36.

29. Monroe S. Kuttner, *Managing the Paperwork Pipeline* (New York: John Wiley & Sons, 1978).

30. Charles A. O'Reilly, III, "Variations in Decision Makers' Use of Information Sources: The Impact of Quality and Accessibility of Information" (mimeograph available from the author, Berkeley: University of California, School of Business Administration, February 1979).

31. Jeffrey Pfeffer, *Organizational Design* (Arlington Heights, Illinois: AHM Publishing Co., 1978), pp. 82-83.

32. Gerald M. Goldhaber, Harry S. Dennis, Gary M. Richetto, and Osmo A. Wiio, *Information Strategies: New Pathways to Corporate Power* (Englewood Cliffs, N.J.: Prentice-Hall, Inc., 1979), pp. 35-36.

33. A. C. Filley, "Committee Management: Guidelines from Social Science Research," *California Management Review,* 13, no. 1 (1970): 13-21.

34. Roberts and O'Reilly, p. 1.

35. Karlene H. Roberts and Charles A. O'Reilly, III, "Some Correlations of Communication Roles in Organizations," *Academy of Management Journal,* 22 (March 1979): 46.

36. Winford E. Holland, "The Special Communicator and His Behavior in Research Organizations: A Key to the Management of Informal Technical Information Flow," *IEEE Transactions on Professional Communication,* Vol. PC-17 (September-December 1974): 48-53.

37. Lewis M. Branscomb, "Information: The Ultimate Frontier," *Science,* 23 (January 12, 1979): 54-57.

38. F. Wilfrid Lancaster, "Whither Libraries? Or, Wither Libraries?" *College & Research Libraries,* 39 (September 1978): 345-57.

APPENDIX I
INFORMATION CONTACT
STUDY QUESTIONNAIRE

QUESTIONNAIRE

Instructions: Please answer the questions in Part I *prior to our interview* by supplying the necessary information in the appropriate blank. The questions in Parts II and III will be asked during our interview and are provided at this time so that you might make notes or consider your responses in advance.

THANKS FOR YOUR HELP!!

PART I

1. Name _____ 2. Age _____
3. Years employed in this library ____ 4. Years in the library profession ____
5. Circle the educational degrees you have received: (a) Bachelor's (b) MLS (c) Subject Master's (d) Doctorate
6. If you are currently taking courses toward another degree, how many hours have you completed? _____ What is the degree? _____

PART II

Professional Activity

7. Are you a member of any professional organizations? If yes, which ones?
8. If you are a member of a professional organization, are you currently serving on any committees? If yes, which ones?

9. Specifically, what professional meetings, workshops, colloquia, etc. did you attend during the past year?

10. Have you presented any papers, given speeches, or served on discussion panels at any of those meetings during the past year? If yes, which ones?

Institutional Activity

11. Are you an *elected* official to any college/university, library or professional organizations? If yes, which ones?

12. Have you served on any college/university committees or advisory groups (not including those in question 11) during the past year? If yes, which ones?

13. Have you served on any library committees or advisory groups (not including those in question 11) during the past year? If yes, which ones?

Communication Activity

14. On an average day, how many memos do you write to other employees in the library?

15. On an average day, how many letters do you write or telephone calls do you make to individuals *outside* the library which are necessary for you to adequately perform your job?

16. On an average day, how many *different* individuals *in the library* do you communicate with (either face-to-face or over the telephone) to obtain information necessary for satisfactory performance on the job?
   (a) professional librarians   (c) college/university faculty
   (b) para-professional staff   (d) other

17. Please name *one* person on whom you *most frequently* rely to obtain information about general operations or conditions in the library.

Research Activity

18. What is your estimate of the size of your personal collection of books and related publications concerning librarianship and/or your other areas of professional interest?

0-10	26-50	101-250
11-25	51-100	251 or more

19. To which journals related to librarianship or your specific professional areas of interest do you subscribe?

20. What journals related to librarianship or your specific professional areas of interest do you regularly scan or have routed to you?

21. How many articles related to librarianship or your specific professional areas of interest do you *read* during an average month (including both journals to which you subscribe and others that came to your attention)?

22. How many articles relating to librarianship or your specific professional areas of interest have you had published during the past two years? What are their titles?
23. Have you published any books within the past two years? If yes, what are their titles?
24. Have you published any book reviews relating to librarianship or your specific professional areas of interest in the last two years? If yes, what were their titles?
25. Have you actively participated in the writing of any reports, studies, or position papers concerning the affairs of the library during the past two years? If yes, what were the titles?
26. Are you currently engaged in the preparation of an article, monograph, book review, or other document for publication? If yes, please describe.

PART III

Instructions: Listed below are a number of typical library decision situations about which many college/university libraries have had to make major decisions (involving two or more library departments) within recent years.

A. Place an "X" before those decision situations that pertained to your library during the past two years.
B. Describe any other major decision situations that are not included in this list but pertained to your library during the past two years beginning with item number 11.
C. In the space provided at the bottom of this page please indicate *for each* decision situation that pertained to your library the person or persons on whom you relied for information (either written documents or personal advice).

1. Participation in OCLC or some cooperative network
2. Automation of circulation
3. Evaluation procedures for librarians
4. Equitable distribution of budget cuts throughout the library
5. Establishment of a library security system
6. Allocation of the acquisitions budget to college/university departments
7. Library staffing requirements or staffing reorganization
8. Creation of a book approval plan

9. Distribution of floor space or work area of the library to various library departments
10. Unionization, terms and conditions of employment
11. Other (please describe)

*　　*　　*　　*　　*　　*　　*　　*　　*　　*　　*　　*　　*　　*　　*

Decision Situation　　　*Name of Person or Persons on Whom Relied for Info*

PART III

Instructions: Listed below are a number of typical library decision situations about which many college/university libraries have had to make major decisions (involving two or more library departments) within recent years.

A. Place an "X" under column A next to those decision situations that you believe pertained to your library during the past two years.
B. Place an "X" under column B next to those decision situations for which you feel satisfied that you *actively* participated in the making of the decision by directly providing (1) written reports, memos, or other documents, OR (2) contributing other information, advice, or opinion.
C. Describe any other major decision situations that have specifically pertained to your library in the past two years not included in items 1-10 beginning with item 11. Indicate for each whether or not you *actively* participated in the making of the decision under column B.

A	B	Decision Situation
		1. Participation in OCLC or some cooperative network
		2. Automation of circulation
		3. Evaluation procedures for librarians
		4. Equitable distribution of budget cuts throughout the library
		5. Establishment of a library security system
		6. Allocation of the acquisitions budget to college/ university departments
		7. Library staffing requirements or staffing reorganization
		8. Creation of a book approval plan
		9. Distribution of floor space or work area of the library to various library departments
		10. Unionization, terms and conditions of employment
		11. Other (please describe)

APPENDIX II
INFORMATION EVALUATION
STUDY QUESTIONNAIRE

QUESTIONNAIRE ON VALUE
OF INFORMATION SOURCES
FOR DECISION MAKING

This questionnaire has been designed to collect data as to *your* preferences for contacting specific types of information sources as input to library decision making. With a better understanding of your preferences for certain types of information for specific decision situations, I hope to be able to develop strategies to improve organizational decision making and information flow.

THANKS: Your assistance in completing this questionnaire is greatly appreciated. Please answer *all* questions, giving your *best* choice as answer to each question. No names are needed so your anonymity is assured.
AGAIN, THANKS FOR YOUR HELP!!!

Dr. Charles R. McClure
School of Library Science
University of Oklahoma
Norman, Oklahoma 73019

PART I BACKGROUND INFORMATION

1. Sex: ( ) Male   ( ) Female   2. Age: _____

3. Which one category BEST describes your administrative responsibilities?
   ( ) Top Administration: Director, Associate Director, Assistant Director
   ( ) Department Head: Supervises at least one other professional
   ( ) Area or Section Head: Supervises only paraprofessionals
   ( ) Nonadministrative: Does not supervise other library employees
4. Which one category BEST describes your *primary* area of responsibility
   in the library?
   ( ) Administrative: Director or Asst.   ( ) Automation/Systems
       Director, or Assoc. Director   ( ) Reference Services
   ( ) Acquisitions   ( ) Collection Development
   ( ) Cataloging   ( ) Special Collections or
                                                    special types of materials
                                                    such as govt. documents,
                                                    microforms, etc.

   ( ) OTHER, Please describe _____
5. Which one category BEST describes your education?
   ( ) Bachelor's degree only
   ( ) Master's degree in library science only
   ( ) Master's degree NOT in library science only, Subject: _____
   ( ) Master's degrees in library science AND subject, Subject: _____
   ( ) Doctorate, Subject: _____
6. How many years of experience have you in present library?
   _____years
7. How many total years of library-related experience have you?
   _____years
8. Circle the number that represents the degree *YOU* believe *YOUR* informational input affects decisions made in the library.

1	2	3	4	5	6	7

   no   some   great
   effect   effect   effect

PART II PREFERENCE FOR INFORMATION SOURCES

Instructions: Listed below in part A is a set of possible decision situations related to a library environment. Read each decision situation and
assume that you have been asked to analyze the situation as it pertains
to your library.

From the list of possible information sources in Part B (next page), place the number (1 through 20) corresponding to that information source you would select for a certain decision situation in the appropriate column below.

Regardless of your basic knowledge for these decision situations *please respond to each situation* by providing your preferences for information sources.

Place the number that corresponds to the selected information source (page 3) under each column for:

First Choice: The information source you would first contact as an aid to analyze the decision situation

Second Choice: The information source you would contact secondly as a possible aid to analyze the decision situation

Last Choice: The information source you would assume to be *least helpful* to analyze the decision situation

A. Decision Situations

First Choice	Second Choice	Decision Situation	Last Choice
―――	―――	A. Automation of circulation	―――
―――	―――	B. Evaluation of candidates for a new position	―――
―――	―――	C. Purchasing books or other materials for the library	―――
―――	―――	D. How to equitably allocate the acquisitions budget	―――
―――	―――	E. How to reorganize the floor space of the library work areas and stacking areas	―――
―――	―――	F. Whether the library should increase or decrease hours of operation	―――
―――	―――	G. Providing on-line data base reference services	―――
―――	―――	H. Establishing or improving the library security system	―――

      I. Implementing copyright procedures
  ——   ——   for the library   ——

      J. Joining a union or collective bargain-
  ——   ——   ing unit   ——

      K. How to equitably evaluate library
  ——   ——   personnel   ——

      L. Joining a cooperative bibliographic
  ——   ——   network   ——

B. List of Information Sources

INTERPERSONAL CONTACT WITH
1. professional staff in the library
2. paraprofessional staff in the library
3. library patrons (users)
4. librarians *outside* the library
5. faculty members
6. vendors, jobbers, salespersons

WRITTEN DOCUMENTS
7. books
8. articles from library-related periodicals or journals
9. book reviews
10. articles from journals NOT related directly to librarianship
11. brochures, advertisements, flyers, etc.
12. reports or statistical information produced by staff members in your library

GROUP OR ORGANIZATIONAL
13. committee or group meetings composed of library staff members
14. committee or group meetings with nonlibrary staff members
15. committee or group meetings of professional organizations (ALA, etc.)
16. continuing education: workshops, sources, seminars, etc.

PERSONAL
17. past experiences
18. personal opinion
19. do some research on my own to analyze decision situation

OTHER: Please describe:
20. _____

BIBLIOGRAPHY

Ackoff, Russell L. "Management Misinformation Systems." *Management Science*, 14 (December 1967): B133-36.

Ackoff, Russell L., et al., *The SCATT Report: A Tentative Idealized Design of a National Scientific Communication and Technology Transfer System.* Philadelphia: The Wharton School, University of Pennsylvania, 1975.

Adams, John R., and Swanson, Lloyd A. "Information Processing Behavior and Estimating Accuracy in Operations Management." *Academy of Management Journal,* 19 (March 1976): 98-110.

Allen, Richard K. *Organizational Management Through Communication.* New York: Harper & Row, 1977.

Allen, T. J. "Information Needs and Uses." In *Annual Review of Information Science and Technology,* vol. 4, pp. 1-29. Ed. Carlos A. Cuadra. Chicago: Encyclopaedia Britannica, 1969.

——. *Managing the Flow of Technology: Technology Transfer and the Dissemination of Technological Information Within the R & D Organization.* Cambridge, Mass.: The M.I.T. Press, 1977.

Allen, T. J., and Cohen, S. I. "Information Flow in Research and Development Laboratories." *Administrative Science Quarterly,* 14 (March 1969): 12-19.

Allen, T. J., Gerstenfeld, A., and Gerstenfeld, P. G. *The Problem of Internal Consulting in Research and Development Organizations.* Washington, D.C.: National Science Foundation, Office of Science Information Service, July 1965.

American Library Directory, 1976-1977. New York: Bowker, 1976.

Andrus, Roman R. "Approaches to Information Evaluation." In *Readings in Management Information Systems,* pp. 103-108. Ed. Gordon B. Davis and Gordon C. Everest. New York: McGraw-Hill, 1976.

Argyris, Chris. "Some Limitations of Rational Man Organization Theory." *Public Administration Review,* 33 (May-June 1973): 253-67.

Artandi, Susan. "Information Concepts and Their Utility." *Journal of the American Society for Information Science,* 24 (July-August 1973): 242-45.

Bacharach, Samuel B., and Aiken, Michael. "Communication in Administrative Bureaucracies." *Academy of Management Journal,* 20 (September 1977): 365-77.

Bavelas, Alex. "Leadership: Man and Function." In *Readings in Managerial Psychology,* pp. 373-80. Ed. Harold J. Leavitt and Louis R. Pondy. Chicago: University of Chicago Press, 1964.

Becker, Selwyn W. "Personality and Effective Communication in the Organization." *Personnel Administration,* 23 (July-August 1964): 28-30.

Bell, Daniel. *The Coming of Post Industrial Society.* New York: Basic Books, 1973.

Boulding, Kenneth. "The Ethics of Rational Decision." *Management Science,* 12 (February 1966): B161-B169.

Branscomb, Lewis M. "Information: The Ultimate Frontier." *Science,* 23 (January 12, 1979): 54-57.

Brittain, J. M. *Information and Its Users.* New York: John Wiley & Sons, 1970.

Carlson, Walter M. "Where Is the Payoff?" *Bulletin of the American Society for Information Science,* 4 (October 1977): 14-15, 17.

Churchman, C. West. "Managerial Acceptance of Scientific Recommendations." In *Information for Decision Making,* p. 442. Ed. Alfred Rappaport. Englewood Cliffs, N.J.: Prentice Hall, 1970.

Connolly, Terry. "Information Processing and Decision Making in Organizations." In *New Directions in Organizational Behavior.* Ed. Barry M. Staw and Gerald R. Salancik. Chicago: St. Clair Press, 1977.

Crane, Diana. "Information Needs and Uses." In *Annual Review of Information Science and Technology,* vol. 6, pp. 3-39. Ed. Carlos A. Cuadra. Washington, D.C.: American Society for Information Science, 1971.

Crawford, Jeffrey, and Healand, Gordon A. "Predecisional Process and Information Seeking in Social Influence." In *Proceedings of the Annual Convention of the American Psychological Association,* pp. 161-162. New York: American Psychological Association, 1971.

Crawford, Susan. "Information Needs and Uses." In *Annual Review of Information Science and Technology,* vol. 13, pp. 61-81. Ed. Martha Williams. White Plains, N.Y.: Knowledge Industries, 1978.

Creighton, J. W., Jolly, J. A., and Denning, S. A. *Enhancement of Research and Development Output Utilization Efficiencies: Linker Concept Methodology in the Technology Transfer Process.* Monterey, Calif.: U. S. Navy Postgraduate School, 1972.

Czepiel, John A. "Patterns of Interorganizational Communications and the Diffusion of a Major Technological Innovation in a Competitive Industrial Community." *Academy of Management Journal,* 18 (March 1975): 6-24.

——. "Word of Mouth Processes in the Diffusion of a Major Technological Innovation." *Journal of Marketing Research,* 11 (May 1974): 172-78.

Dance, F. E. X. "The Concept of Communication." *Journal of Communication,* 20 (September 1970): 201-10.

Dewhirst, Dudley H. "Influence of Perceived Information Sharing Norms on Communication Channel Utilization." *Academy of Management Journal,* 14 (September 1971): 305-15.

Drucker, Peter F. *Management: Tasks, Responsibilities, Practices.* New York: Harper & Row, 1973.

Durr, W. T. "Information as a Source of Bureaucratic Power in the Political Decision Making Process." In *The Information Age in Perspective: Proceedings of the ASIS Annual Meeting,* vol. 15, pp. 119-22. Comp. Everett H. Brenner. White Plains, N.Y.: Knowledge Industries, 1978.

Ebert, Ronald J., and Mitchell, Terence R. *Organizational Decision Processes: Concepts and Analysis.* New York: Crane Russak & Company, 1975.

Eden, Colin, and Harris, John. *Management Decision and Decision Analysis.* New York: John Wiley & Sons, 1975.

Farace, Richard V., and Danowski, James A. *Analyzing Human Communication Networks in Organizations Applications to Management Problems.* East Lansing: Michigan State University, Department of Communication, 1973. ERIC Document no. 099943.

Farr, Richard S. *Knowledge Linkers and the Flow of Education Information.* Stanford, Calif.: ERIC Clearinghouse on Educational Media and Technology, 1969. ERIC Document no. 032438.

Ferguson, Thomas S. *Mathematical Statistics: A Decision Theoretic Approach.* New York: Academic Press, 1967.

Filley, A. C. "Committee Management: Guidelines from Social Science Research." *California Management Review,* 13, no. 1 (1970): 13-21.

Gersberger, P. G., and Allen, T. J. "Criteria Used by Research and Development Engineers in the Selection of an Information Source." *Journal of Applied Psychology,* 52 (August 1968): 272-79.

Glock, C., and Menzel, Herbert. *The Flow of Information Among Scientists: Problems, Opportunities and Research Questions.* New York: Columbia University, Bureau of Applied Social Research, 1958.

Goldhaber, Gerald M., Dennis, Harry S., Richetto, Gary M., and Wiio, Osmo A. *Information Strategies: New Pathways to Corporate Power.* Englewood Cliffs, N.J.: Prentice Hall, 1979.

Goldhaber, Gerald M., et al. "Organizational Communication: 1978." *Human Communication Research,* 5 (Fall 1978): 76-96.

Goldhar, Joel D., Bragaw, Louis K., and Schwartz, Jules J. "Information Flows, Management Styles, and Technological Innovation." *IEEE Transactions on Engineering Management,* EM 23 (February 1976): 51-62.

Graves, Clare W. "Levels of Existence: An Open System Theory of Values." *Journal of Humanistic Psychology,* 10 (Fall 1970): 131-55.

Greenwood, Frank. "Your New Job in Information Management Resource." *Journal of Systems Management,* 30 (April 1970): 24-27.

Haige, J., Aiken, M., and Marrett, C. B. "Organization Structure and Communications." *American Sociological Review,* 36 (1971): 860-71.

Hall, Homer J. "Values in the Evaluation of Information." Paper distributed by author at the Annual Conference of the American Association for Information Science, New York, November 1978 (mimeograph).

Havelock, Ronald G. *Planning for Innovation through Dissemination and Utilization of Knowledge.* Ann Arbor, Mich.: Center for Research on Utilization of Scientific Knowledge, 1969.

——. "Research on the Utilization of Knowledge." In *Information for Action,* p. 97. Ed. Manfred Kochen. New York: Academic Press, 1975.

Hersberg, Frederick. *Work and the Nature of Man.* Cleveland, Ohio: World Publishing Company, 1966.

Hodge, D. M., and Nelson, G. H. *Biological Laboratories Communication.* Fort Detrick, Frederick, Md.: U. S. Army Biological Laboratories, Technical Information Division, 1965.

Holland, Winford E. "Information Potential: A Concept of the Importance of Information Sources in a Research and Development Environment." *Journal of Communication,* 22 (June 1972): 142-58.

——. "The Special Communicator and His Behavior in Research Organizations: A Key to the Management of Informal Technical Information Flow." *IEEE Transactions on Professional Communication,* PC-17 (September-December 1974): 48-53.

Horton, Forest Woody, Jr. "A Government Occupational Standard for Information Manager." *Information Manager,* 1 (March-April 1979): 34-36.

——. *How to Harness Information Resources: A Systems Approach.* Cleveland, Ohio: Association for Systems Management, 1974.

Horton, Woody W., Jr. "Information Resources Management, Fad or Fact?" *Journal of Systems Management,* 28 (December 1977): 6-9.

Ilchman, Warren F., and Uphoff, Norman Thomas. *The Political Economy of Change.* Berkeley: University of California Press, 1969.

Inkeles, Alex. "Problems in the Utilization of Data for Policy Making." In *Information for Action,* p. 173. Ed. Manfred Kochen. New York: Academic Press, 1975.

Jackson, Eugene. "Communication Practices in Complex Organizations." *Journal of Social Issues,* 7, no. 3 (1951): 37.

Janis, Irving L., and Mann, Leon. *Decision Making.* New York: The Free Press, 1977.

Jones, Graham. "This Incredible Stream of Garbage: The Library Journals 1876-1975." *The Indexer,* 10 (April 1976): 9-14.

Kaplan, Abraham. *The Conduct of Inquiry.* Scranton, Pa.: Chandler Publishing Company, 1964.

Kaplan, Louis. "The Literature of Participation: From Optimism to Realism." *College & Research Libraries* (November 1975): 473-79.

Kasperson, Conrad J. "An Analysis of the Relationship Between Information Sources and Creativity in Scientists and Engineers." *Human Communication Research,* 4 (Winter 1978): 113-19.

Kast, Fremont E., and Rosenzweig, James E. "General Systems Theory: Applications for Organization and Management." *Academy of Management Journal,* 15 (December 1972): 447-68.

——. *Organization and Management: A Systems Approach.* 2nd ed. New York: McGraw-Hill, 1974.

Katz, Elihu, and Lazarsfeld, Paul F. *Personal Influences: The Part Played by People in the Flow of Mass Communications.* Glencoe, Ill.: The Free Press, 1955.

Katzer, Jeffrey, Cook, Kenneth H., and Crouch, Wayne W. *Evaluating Information: A Guide for Social Science Research.* Reading, Mass.: Addison-Wesley, 1978.

Kernan, Jerome B., and Mojena, Richard. "Information Utilization and Personality." *Journal of Communication,* 23 (September 1973): 325.

Kies, Cosette Nell. *Unofficial Relations, Personal Reliance, Informal Influence, Communications, and Library Staff: A Sociometric Investigation of Three Medium-Sized Public Libraries.* Ph.D. diss., Columbia University, 1977.

Klemmer, E. T., and Synder, F. W. "Measurement of Time Spent Communicating." *Journal of Communication,* 22 (June 1972): 142-58.

Koontz, Harold, and O'Donnell, Cyril. *Management: A Systems and Contingency Analysis of Managerial Functions.* 6th ed. New York: McGraw-Hill, 1976.

Kuttner, Monroe S. *Managing the Paperwork Pipeline.* New York: John Wiley & Sons, 1978.

Lancaster, F. Wilfrid. "Whither Libraries? Or, Wither Libraries?" *College & Research Libraries,* 39 (September 1978): 345-57.

Lasswell, Harold D. "Constraints on the Use of Knowledge in Decision Making." In *Information for Action,* pp. 161-70. Ed. Manfred Kochen. New York: Academic Press, 1975.

Leother, Herman J., and McTavish, Donald G. *Inferential Statistics for Sociologists.* Boston: Allyn and Bacon, 1974.

Library Statistics of Colleges and Universities: Fall 1973. 2 vols. Washington, D.C.: National Center for Education Statistics, 1976.

Likert, Rensis, and Likert, Jane Gibson. *New Ways of Managing Conflict.* New York: McGraw-Hill, 1976.

Lin, Nan. *Foundations of Social Research.* New York: McGraw-Hill, 1976.

Lindgren, B. W. *Elements of Decision Theory.* New York: Macmillan Company, 1971.

Littell, Ramon C., and Folks, J. Leroy. "Asymptotic Optimality of Fisher's Method of Combining Independent Tests." *Journal of the American Statistical Association,* 66 (December 1971): 802-6.

Lowi, Theodore. "Government and Politics: Blurring of Sector Lines, Rise of New Elites." In *Information Technology: Some Critical Implications for Decision Makers,* pp. 131-48. New York: The Conference Board, 1972.

Luthans, Fred. *Introduction to Management: A Contingency Approach.* New York: McGraw-Hill, 1976.

March, James G., and Simon, Herbert A. *Organizations.* New York: John Wiley & Sons, 1958.

Marchant, Maurice P. *Participative Management in Academic Libraries.* Westport, Conn.: Greenwood Press, 1976.

Maslow, A. H. "A Theory of Human Motivation." *Psychological Review,* 50 (1943): 270-96.

McClure, Charles R. *Academic Librarians' Contact with Information Sources and Library Decision Making.* Ph.D. diss., Rutgers University, 1977.

——. "Academic Librarians, Information Sources, and Shared Decision Making." *Journal of Academic Librarianship,* 6 (March 1980): 9-15.

——. "Categories of Information Sources and Library Decision Making." In *The Information Age in Perspective: Proceedings of the ASIS Annual Meeting, 1978,* pp. 213-16. Comp. Everett H. Brenner. White Plains, N.Y.: Knowledge Industries, 1978.

——. "The Planning Process: Strategies for Action." *College & Research Libraries,* 39 (November 1978): 456-66.

Menzel, Herbert. "Informal Communication in Science, Its Advantages and Its Formal Analogues." In *Toward a Theory of Librarianship,* pp. 404-14. Ed. Conrad Rawski. Metuchen, N.J.: Scarecrow Press, 1973.

——. "The Information Needs of Current Scientific Research." *Library Quarterly,* 34 (January 1964): 4-19.

Miles, Raymond E. *Theories of Management: Implications for Organizational Behavior and Development.* New York: McGraw-Hill, 1975.

Miller, George A. "The Magical Number Seven, Plus or Minus Two: Some Limits on Our Capacity for Processing Information." *Psychological Review,* 63 (March 1956): 81-98.

Miller, Gerald R. "The Current Status of Theory and Research in Interpersonal Communication."*Human Communication Research,* 4 (Winter 1978): 164-78.

Mintzberg, Henry. "Review of *New Science of Management Decision." Administrative Science Quarterly,* 22 (June 1977): 342-50.

Mulder, Mauk, and Wilke, Henk. "Participation and Power Equalization." *Organizational Behavior & Human Performance,* 5 (September 1970): 430-48.

Nunally, Jim C. *Psychometric Theory.* New York: McGraw-Hill, 1967.

Ogden, C. K., and Richards, I. A. *The Meaning of Meaning.* London: Routledge & Kegan Paul, 1949.

O'Reilly, Charles A., III. *The Intentional Distortion of Information in Organizational Communication: A Laboratory and Field Investigation.* Berkeley: Institute of Industrial Relations, University of California, 1975. NTIS Document No. AD-A020330/7GI.

——. "Variation in Decision Makers' Use of Information Sources: The Impact of Quality and Accessibility of Information." Berkeley: University of California, School of Business Administration, February 1979 (mimeograph).

Paisley, William J. *Behavioral Studies of Scientific Information Flow: An Appendix on Method.* Stanford, Calif.: Stanford University, 1969.

——. "Information Needs and Uses." In *Annual Review of Information Science and Technology,* vol. 3, pp. 1-30. Ed. Carlos A. Cuadra. Chicago: Encyclopaedia Britannica, 1968.

Pelz, Donald C., and Andrews, Frank M. *Scientists in Organizations: Productive Climates for Research and Development.* New York: John Wiley & Sons, 1966.

Peterfreund, Emanual. *Information, Systems, and Psychoanalysis.* New York: International Universities Press, 1971.

Pfeffer, Jeffrey. *Organizational Design.* Arlington Heights, Illinois: AHM Publishing Corporation, 1978.

Plate, Kenneth H. *Management Personnel in Libraries: A Theoretical Model for Analysis.* Rockaway, N.J.: American Faculty Press, 1970.

Porat, Avner M., and Haas, John A. "Information Effects on Decision Making." *Behavioral Science,* 14 (March 1969): 98-104.

Porat, Marc Uri. *The Information Economy,* 7 vols. Washington, D.C.: U. S., Department of Commerce, 1977.

Porter, Lyman W., and Roberts, Karlene H. "Communication in Organizations." In *Handbook of Industrial and Organizational Psychology,* pp. 1553-589. Ed. Marvin D. Dunnette. Chicago: Rand McNally, 1976.

Price, Derek de Solla. "Some Aspects of 'World Brain' Notions." In *Information for Action,* pp. 177-92. Ed. Manfred Kochen. New York: Academic Press, 1975.

Richmond, Virginia. "The Relationship Between Opinion Leadership and Information Acquisition." *Human Communication Research,* 4 (Fall 1977): 38-43.

Roberts, Karlene H., and O'Reilly, Charles A., III. *Communication Roles in Organizations: Some Potential Antecedents and Consequences.* Berkeley: Institute of Industrial Relations, University of California, 1975. NTIS Document no. A013 676/2GA.

——. *Interpersonal Communication, Personnel Ratings, and Systematic Performance Characteristics in Organizations.* Berkeley: University of California, Institute of Industrial Relations, 1975. NTIS Document no. AD A013874/7GA.

——. "Measuring Organizational Communication." *Journal of Applied Psychology,* 59 (June 1974): 321-26.

——. *Organizations as Communication Structures: An Empirical-Theoretical Approach.* Berkeley: Institute of Industrial Relations, University of California, 1975. NTIS Document no. Ad-A013675/4GA.

——. "Organizations as Communication Structures: An Empirical Approach." *Human Communication Research,* 4 (Summer 1978): 283-93.

——. "Organizational Theory and Organizational Communication: A Communication Failure?" *Human Relations,* 27 (May 1974): 501-24.

——. "Some Correlates of Communication Roles in Organizations." *Academy of Management Journal,* 22 (March 1979): 42-57.

Roeach, Milton. *The Open and Closed Mind.* New York: Basic Books, 1960.

Rogers, Everett M., and Rogers, Rekha Agarwala. *Communication in Organizations.* New York: The Free Press, 1976.

Roscoe, John T. *Fundamental Research Statistics for Behavioral Sciences.* 2nd ed. New York: Holt, Rinehart and Winston, 1975.

Rubenstein, A. H. "Timing and Form of Researcher Needs for Technical Information." *Journal of Chemical Documentation,* 2 (January 1962): 28-31.

Ruterbusch, Milton. "Information Management in the Modern Automated Office." *Information & Records Management* (April 1979): 28-34.

Sabatier, Paul. " The Acquisition and Utilization of Technical Information by Administrative Agencies." *Administrative Science Quarterly,* 23 (September 1978): 396-417.

Simon, Herbert A. *Administrative Behavior.* 3rd ed. New York: The Free Press, 1976.

———. *The New Science of Management Decision.* Rev. ed. Englewood Cliffs, N.J.: Prentice Hall, 1977.

Smith, A. G. *Communication and Status: The Dynamics of a Research Center.* Eugene: University of Oregon, Center for the Advanced Study of Educational Administration, 1966.

SPSS: Statistical Package for the Social Sciences. 2nd ed. New York: McGraw-Hill, 1975.

Starck, Kenneth. "Values and Information Sources Preferences." *Journal of Communication,* 23 (March 1973): 74-85.

Swisher, Robert Dean. *Professional Communication Behavior of Academic Librarians Holding Membership in the American Library Association.* Ph.D. diss., University of Indiana, 1975.

Tagliacozzo, Renata, Kochen, Manfred, and Everett, William. "The Use of Information by Decision Makers in Public Service Organizations." *In* Communications for Decision Makers: Proceedings of the American Society for Information Science,* vol. 8, pp. 53-57. Ed. Jeanne B. North. Westport, Conn.: Greenwood Press, 1971.

Thayer, Lee O. "On Theory-Building in Communication: Some Conceptual Problems." *Journal of Communication,* 13 (December 1963): 217-35.

Tobias, Audrey Sylvia. "The Yule Curve, Describing Periodical Citations by Freshman." *Journal of Academic Librarianship,* 1 (March 1975): 14-16.

Trueswell, Richard. "Some Behavioral Patterns of Library Users: The 80/20 Rule." *Wilson Library Bulletin,* 43 (January 1969): 458-61.

Uphoff, Norman Thomas. "Information as a Political Resource." In *Humanization of Knowledge in the Social Sciences,* pp. 40-57. Ed. Pauline Atherton. Syracuse: N.Y.: Syracuse University, School of Library Science, 1972.

U. S., Federal Paperwork Commission. *Reference Manual for Program and Information Officials.* 2 vols. Washington, D.C.: U.S. Government Printing Office, 1978.

Vickery, B. C. *Information Systems.* Hamden, Conn.: Archon Books, 1973.

von Neumann, John, and Mergenstern, O. *Theory of Games and Economic Behavior,* 3rd ed. Princeton, N.J.: Princeton University Press, 1944.

Vroom, Victor, and Yetton, Phillip W. *Leadership and Decision Making.* Pittsburgh: University of Pittsburgh Press, 1973.

Wald, Abraham. *Statistical Decision Functions.* Bronx: Chelsea Publishing Company, 1971.

Weisbod, B. A. "Comparing Utility Functions in Efficiency Terms." *American Economic Record,* 67 (December 1977): 991-95.

Wells, William D., and Sheth, Jagdish N. "Factor Analysis." In *Handbook of Marketing Research.* ed. Robert Ferber. New York: McGraw-Hill, 1974.

Whittesmore, Bruce J., and Yovits, M. C. "A Generalized Conceptual Development for the Analysis and Flow of Information." *Journal of the American Society for Information Science,* 24 (May-June 1973): 221-31.

Wilkin, Anne. "Personal Roles and Barriers in Information Transfer." In *Advances in Librarianship,* vol. 7, pp. 257-97. Ed. Melvin J. Voigt and Michael H. Harris. New York: Academic Press, 1977.

Witka, D. K., ed. *Handbook of Measurement and Assessment in Sciences,* 2nd ed. Reading, Mass.: Addison-Wesley, 1968.

Zmud, Robert W. "An Empirical Investigation of the Dimensionality of the Concept of Information." *Decision Science,* 9 (April 1978): 187-95.

INDEX